WHAT YOUR COLLEAGUES

What an amazing, practical resource to support teach... ...
strengthening communication and building partnerships with parents to support student learning in mathematics! Positioning parents as partners underscores that together we can ensure all students see themselves as thinkers and doers of mathematics.

Trena L. Wilkerson
President of the National Council of Teachers of Mathematics (2021–2023)
Professor of Mathematics Education
Baylor University
Waco, TX

Parents send us the best they have each day, their children. The dreams, plans, and aspirations for a better and brighter future for their children are entrusted to educators, with the hope that we will do all we can to prepare them. This powerful resource is filled with insights from parents, practical guidance, and tools to help educators truly build the much-needed partnerships with parents to change the narrative.

John W. Staley
Chair of the U.S. National Commission on Mathematics Instruction (2018–2020)
President of NCSM Leadership in Mathematics Education (2015–2017)
Coordinator
Baltimore County Public Schools
Baltimore, MD

This book is a must-read for any elementary educator who wants to empower their students and families to love math! It is a how-to guide in helping YOU as an educator improve your best practices. This book will encourage you to hit the ground running and initiate the change we need for today's 21st century math instruction!

Katelin Shepler
First Grade Teacher
Folsom Cordova Unified School District
Folsom, CA

Parents are assets and critical partners to student's mathematical success! *Partnering With Parents in Elementary School Math* provides school educators and leaders with just the right strategies, exemplars, and structures to honor the strengths, knowledge, and skills that all families bring to support their child's mathematical journey. This is the book I've been waiting for!

Cathery Yeh
Assistant Professor
Chapman University
Orange, CA

Parents and caregivers play an instrumental role in the mathematical success of their children, but many may be surprised by current mathematical teaching practices. Navigating this sometimes new territory is particularly demanding for families thrust into active teaching roles through online education. As the authors emphasize, we need a team approach that will support each and every child. This must-read book bridges home and school with ways to share mindsets and language, build coherent structures, and make mathematics instruction a positive, high-quality, and inclusive learning experience.

Karen S. Karp and Sarah B. Bush
Co-authors of *The Math Pact*

This is a great easy-to-implement resource for teachers who want to engage in effective communication with parents and help them make sense of their child's mathematics learning experience.

Kristopher J. Childs
President
K Childs Solutions
Winter Garden, FL

Families are crucial partners in children's education, and educators need strategies to ensure partnership works. This is especially true in elementary mathematics education, where content may be unfamiliar or presented in new ways—ultimately leading to confusion between home and school. This guide supports the crucial work of opening communication channels, aligning educators' and families' efforts toward the same goals.

Ilana Seidel Horn
Professor of Mathematics Education and Author of *Motivated: Designing Mathematics Classrooms Where Students Want to Join In*
Nashville, TN

Who are our most powerful—and yet underserved—partners in math learning? Parents. In this compelling book, the authors help educators envision what vibrant parent–school partnerships can do for math education, then equip us with the skills and tools we need to build these relationships.

B. Michelle Rinehart
Educational Consultant
HowWeTeach Consulting
Fort Davis, TX

Teachers spend a great deal of time planning for effective mathematics instruction; this book offers practical and actionable ways for teachers and schools to maximize the work they're doing around elementary mathematics by bringing parents in as stronger partners in this work.

Kristine Gettelman
Early Learning Mathematics Specialist
Mathematics Institute of Wisconsin
Milwaukee, WI

This book provides step-by-step guidance for schools to facilitate effective communication with parents while still giving the schools choices in how and what communication will look like. A must-read to build equitable practices that impact all students.

Lori Mueller
President of the Iowa Council of Teachers of Mathematics
Math Consultant
Great Prairie Area Education Agency
West Point, IA

This book offers suggestions, strategies, and structures elementary teachers need and want to educate and inform parents. The authors' work is comprehensive and very practical, and it thoughtfully provides teachers with incredible ready-to-use ideas for promoting math home-to-school connections.

Kristen Mangus
Mathematics Support Teacher
Howard County Public School System
Howard County, MD

Look no further for an invaluable resource as a reference or professional book study to enhance the parent/community engagement portion of your school's mission or improvement plan. Kreisberg and Beyranevand have created a powerful how-to guide for teachers and school leaders to create and strengthen partnerships with parents, families, and caregivers in service of children's mathematics learning.

Paul Gray
President of NCSM Leadership in Mathematics Education (2021–2023)
Dallas, TX

PARTNERING
WITH PARENTS
IN ELEMENTARY SCHOOL
Math

HILARY KREISBERG · MATTHEW L. BEYRANEVAND

PARTNERING WITH PARENTS
IN ELEMENTARY SCHOOL
Math

A GUIDE FOR TEACHERS AND LEADERS

CORWIN **Mathematics**

CORWIN
A SAGE Publishing Company

For information:

Corwin
A SAGE Company
2455 Teller Road
Thousand Oaks, California 91320
(800) 233–9936
www.corwin.com

SAGE Publications Ltd.
1 Oliver's Yard
55 City Road
London, EC1Y 1SP
United Kingdom

SAGE Publications India Pvt. Ltd.
B 1/I 1 Mohan Cooperative
Industrial Area
Mathura Road, New Delhi 110 044
India

SAGE Publications Asia-Pacific Pte. Ltd.
18 Cross Street #10–10/11/12
China Square Central
Singapore 048423

Publisher, Corwin Mathematics: Erin Null
Associate Content Development
    Editor: Jessica Vidal
Production Editor: Tori Mirsadjadi
Copy Editor: Christina West
Typesetter: Integra
Proofreader: Susan Schon
Indexer: Integra
Cover Designer: Lysa Becker
Marketing Manager: Maura Sullivan

Library of Congress Cataloging-in-Publication Data

Names: Kreisberg, Hilary, 1988 - author. | Beyranevand, Matthew L., 1977- author.
Title: Partnering with parents in elementary school math : a guide for teachers and leaders / Hilary Kreisberg and Matthew L. Beyranevand.
Description: Thousand Oaks, California : Corwin, [2021]
Identifiers: LCCN 2020050055 | ISBN 9781071810866 (paperback) | ISBN 9781071810903 (adobe pdf) | ISBN 9781071810873 (ebook) | ISBN 9781071810897 (ebook)
Subjects: LCSH: Mathematics--Study and teaching--Parent participation. | Mathematics--Study and teaching (Elementary) | Parent-teacher relationships.
Classification: LCC QA135.6 .K745 2021 | DDC 372.7--dc23
LC record available at https://lccn.loc.gov/2020050055

This book is printed on acid-free paper.

SUSTAINABLE
FORESTRY
INITIATIVE
Certified Chain of Custody
Promoting Sustainable Forestry
www.sfiprogram.org
SFI-01268

21 22 23 24 25 10 9 8 7 6 5 4 3 2 1

Contents

Chapter 1 icon source: Enis Aksoy/iStock.com; Chapter 2 icon source: PeterSnow/iStock.com.

Chapter 3 icon source: rambo182/iStock.com; *Chapter 4 icon source:* Momento Design/iStock.com; *Chapter 5 icon source:* Momento Design/iStock.com.

Visit the companion website at
**resources.corwin.com/partneringwithparents/
elementary**
for downloadable resources.

Chapter 6 icon source: Enis Aksoy/iStock.com.

Acknowledgments

Collectively, we would like to thank all of the educators who took time out of their day to interview with us and respond to our surveys. This book would be nothing without your input, experiences, and ideas. We also want to acknowledge the hundreds of parents who over the years have committed time to interviewing with us and responding to our surveys. Your perspectives have allowed us to step into your shoes and help other educators understand what it's like to be a parent of a child learning math today. We can only improve how we help parents if we first understand their experiences. We would also like to recognize the reviewers who offered feedback and suggestions that pushed us to consider more ways to make this work accessible and meaningful. Finally, we must thank our editors, Erin Null and Jessica Vidal, for their unwavering dedication to this work. Your ability to bring out the best in our work helped make this book what it is. Know that we consider you co-authors.

— Hilary and Matthew

First and foremost I must thank Matthew, my partner in crime, for his unconditional friendship and his collaboration on this book. I would also like to acknowledge my husband, Robert, who has watched me pour my heart and soul into this work, undoubtedly missing date nights, dinners, and time focused on family. Your patience and unconditional love helped make this book a reality. I'd also like to thank my parents, Jay and Cindy, and sister, Mandy, for always supporting me and my work. I dedicate this book to my Grandma Shirley, who was and still is my guiding light.

— Hilary

My wife, Valerie, is a saint and played a huge role in the creation of the book. There are a few other people who need to be acknowledged for their impact on me and this book: Mike Horesh, Dr. Silk, Gayle Bateman, Andrew Wise, Glen Hansard, Steven Normandin, Tovak, Linda Hirsch, and Uncle Mo. Finally, major props to the brilliant Hilary. This book was your baby and I was happy to be along for the ride!

— Matthew

PUBLISHER'S ACKNOWLEDGMENTS

Corwin gratefully acknowledges the contributions of the following reviewers:

Nicole Bell
Fifth Grade Teacher/Math Coach
Instructor at Queen's University
Nova Scotia, Canada

Rebecca Evans
Grades 3–5 Math Teacher Leader
Lincoln Public Schools
Lincoln, NE

Kristine Gettelman
Early Learning Mathematics Specialist
Mathematics Institute of Wisconsin
Milwaukee, WI

Kristen Mangus
Mathematics Support Teacher
Howard County Public School System
Howard County, MD

Jacqueline Mickle
Math Consultant
Halton Catholic District School Board
Ontario, Canada

Ruth Harbin Miles
Author, Educational Consultant
Mary Baldwin University
Staunton, VA

Lori Mueller
President of the Iowa Council of Teachers of Mathematics
Math Consultant
Great Prairie Area Education Agency
West Point, IA

Deborah Nalywaiko
First Grade Teacher
Ontario, Canada

B. Michelle Rinehart
Educational Consultant
HowWeTeach Consulting
Fort Davis, TX

Katelin Shepler
First Grade Teacher
Folsom Cordova Unified School District
Folsom, CA

About the Authors

Dr. Hilary Kreisberg is the Director of the Center for Mathematics Achievement and Assistant Professor of Mathematics Education at Lesley University in Cambridge, Massachusetts. She serves as president of the Boston Area Mathematics Specialists organization and is co-author of the book *Adding Parents to the Equation: Understanding Your Child's Elementary School Math (2019)*. Hilary is also a Global Math Project ambassador, reviewer for the National Council of Teachers of Mathematics (NCTM) *Mathematics Teacher* journal, and a curriculum and product developer. She began her career as an elementary teacher and later became a K–5 math coach to be able to support other teachers in their understanding and teaching of mathematics.

Hilary has been featured on NPR Boston (WBUR) Radio and CBS Boston (WBZ) news and in the *Wall Street Journal*, the *Washington Post*, *Education Weekly*, *Boston Magazine*, and the *Lowell Sun*. She is a frequent national, regional, and local speaker and has won over $2 million in federal and private funding for mathematics education research.

She holds a bachelor's degree in mathematics, a master's degree in teaching, and a doctorate in educational leadership and curriculum development. She is a certified U.S. Math Recovery® Intervention Specialist, is also endorsed to teach Sheltered English Immersion (SEI) learners, and holds both special education and mathematics licensure. For fun, Hilary likes to do Zumba and play chess.

Twitter: @Dr_Kreisberg
Website: www.lesley.edu/center/math-achievement

Dr. Matthew L. Beyranevand is the K–12 Mathematics Department Coordinator for the Chelmsford Public Schools in Massachusetts. Matthew is an ambassador for the Global Math Project, consults on the creation of mathematics curriculum, and is a member of the Massachusetts STEM Advisory Council. He also serves as an adjunct professor of mathematics and education at the University of Massachusetts at Lowell and Fitchburg State University. He is the author of the book *Teach Math Like This, Not Like That* and co-author of the book *Adding Parents to the Equation: Understanding Your Child's Elementary School Math*.

Twitter: @MathwithMatthew
Website: www.mathwithmatthew.com

Introduction

*At the end of the day, the most overwhelming key to a child's
success is the positive involvement of parents.*
—Jane D. Hull

Imagine this: a student brings home an assignment on using area models to solve some computational problems. The first problem is 13 × 6. The child has forgotten what they did in class that day and asks their parent for help. "What the heck is an area model?" asks the guardian. The child tries their best to explain: "It is a box, and you put numbers inside it for multiplication." The parent immediately responds, "That's not how I learned how to do it." The child tries to show what they remember from class, yet the process is taking far too long for the busy parent. The parent grabs a piece of paper and says, "Just do it this way: 3 times 6 is 18. The 8 goes here and you carry the 1; 6 times 1 is 6 plus 1 is 7. The answer is 78. See?" Phrases like "Ugh, this is why I hate math" and "Why aren't they learning it how we learned it?" are muttered by all the family members. How did it come to this?

This story, which happens often, has become an accepted "norm" among many families. Stories like these have been portrayed as typical homelife "woes" and broadcast as scenes in movies and television shows. And while it is easy for us educators to experience frustration when we hear these stories, we cannot blame parents for their lack of knowledge about mathematics instruction or for their attitudes and outlook on why we are teaching math the way we are today. So, what is the real issue behind this opening story? For us, it is about *who* is taking responsibility for educating the parents.

Ultimately, the current reality is that many students have been positioned (inadvertently) as chiefly responsible for parents' education about math instruction when it must be the school's job to do this. By not deliberately enacting a plan for educators to take on this leadership position, we have effectively relegated the responsibility to students. It is our role as educators and school leaders to empower parents and engage them in their child's mathematics learning journey to help move our goals forward.

WHY THIS BOOK NOW?

In 2019, we published *Adding Parents to the Equation: Understanding Your Child's Elementary School Math*, a book geared for parents and caregivers of elementary-aged children meant to help them better understand why the way we teach mathematics today differs from how they learned it. It helps parents and caregivers learn to speak our (the educators') mathematical language and offers resources and suggestions for how parents can help their learners at home.

The response from parents was overwhelmingly positive, but more impressive was the response from teachers and school leaders. Many found the book a helpful resource for better understanding the content themselves and determining suggestions they might offer families for fun ways to incorporate mathematics at home. Our attempt at repairing the home-to-school connection had certainly begun. While there are some suggestions in that book that teachers and school leaders could use when working with parents, we believe there needs to be an entirely *separate* book for teachers and leaders that solely focuses on the "how-to" of family engagement in mathematics at the elementary level.

Communicating with parents is more than simply telling them how to do the math we teach today. It also means informing them about why we have shifted our instruction, what their child(ren) will be learning in math, how they can support their children's learning, and much more. To effectively involve parents as key stakeholders and partners, teachers and school leaders must be equipped with resources, tools, and strategies. This book is written to offer suggestions, exemplars, and structures that elementary school educators and leaders can use to educate and engage families in supporting their child's mathematics journey.

Note: Throughout the book, we use the term *parents*. This term includes guardians, caregivers, and anyone who supports mathematics learning at home and/or outside of school.

We all know that parental involvement is critical for our children. Study after study shows us that there is a strong relationship between parental involvement and children's self-efficacy in mathematics and ultimately improvement in their mathematical achievement (Chiu & Xihua, 2008; Fan & Williams, 2010). Yet for some reason, we (the education field at large) have failed to properly address parents and families as the important stakeholders they are. While our teaching practices have adapted and leaders and teachers together have spent an abundance of time, money, and support learning about and implementing new standards, we haven't put nearly as much effort into helping parents understand these shifts. As a result, a large majority of parents of elementary-aged children are left feeling unable to help their children in math or are inadvertently passing on their own math anxieties to their children.

Lessons Learned From the COVID-19 Coronavirus Pandemic

In late 2019, a novel coronavirus (COVID-19) began to spread throughout the Eastern Hemisphere. Little did we know in early 2020 that a global pandemic was around the corner and would cause nearly all schools throughout the world to close with no time to prepare. Ultimately, most schools were forced to enact a distance learning model, which showcased the vast inequities that exist within our school systems—especially within the United States.

At this time of crisis, every stakeholder was unprepared for this event. Parents, in particular, had to quickly become their child's teacher. New memes and social media posts started to pop up highlighting parents' misunderstanding or lack of understanding about mathematics instruction today. We observed many parents undoing many of the strategies developed during the year, sometimes deliberately and sometimes without even knowing it. In fact, one parent told us, "I skipped through all of the nonsense and went right to showing my son the shortcut methods." We can only wonder whether comments like this parent's would have been different if proper structures had been in place prior to the pandemic.

As the pandemic unfolded, more and more parents began teaching their children procedurally to help them "catch up," and some teachers and school leaders were backpedaling to communicate with parents to offer better support. We couldn't help but wonder: *What if we had better prepared parents? What if proactive communication practices were already in place? What if many of the structures we will discuss in this book had been previously established?* It is critical that we partner with parents from the beginning of the school year, and throughout it, so that we are better prepared for any eventuality.

> A large majority of parents of elementary-aged children are left feeling unable to help their children in math or are inadvertently passing on their own math anxieties to their children.

EXAMINING YOUR CORE BELIEFS

In order to partner with parents, you must first believe that *all* parents are assets to you. Take a moment and consider whether you truly believe a child's family is essential to the child's success. Do you honestly recognize the strengths, knowledge, and skills that *all* families bring? Or are there some families you believe are obstacles to a child's success? Do you see weakness, lack of knowledge, and lack of skills that ultimately have you writing off some families as helpful?

According to Henderson and colleagues, your core beliefs about families can impact your ability to build successful partnerships with them (Henderson, Mapp, Johnson, & Davies, 2007; Mapp, Carver, & Lander, 2017). Henderson et al. (2007) determined that there are essential core beliefs that all school leaders, teachers, and other educators should adopt.

Core Beliefs About Families

1. All families have dreams for their children and want the best for them.
2. All families have the capacity to support their children's learning.
3. Families and school staff are equal partners.
4. The responsibility for cultivating and sustaining partnerships among school, home, and community rests primarily with school staff, especially school leaders.

How many of these core beliefs do you share? It is critical that you examine your own beliefs and identify ways to view *all* families as partners if you don't currently share that view.

WHAT ROLE HAVE YOU PLAYED?

Take a moment and think about what you and your colleagues have done in the past (or currently do) to inform parents about the ways in which we instruct mathematics today.

Hopefully these guiding questions have made you think of all the ways you already support parents in math. The first step is acknowledging all that you already do well. We often get so trapped in thinking about what we don't do or could do better that we sometimes forget all that we are already doing.

Now, take some time to reflect and document what you personally have done to inform parents about how math is taught today. Then, document what others in your school or district have done, perhaps those who hold other roles or even those who share the same roles.

Think About the Following

- What have you done to make sure parents understand the math you or your teachers teach?
- How do you communicate with parents about mathematics?
  - How often do you communicate with parents specifically about mathematics?
  - How consistent and equitable is your communication about mathematics with your colleagues' communication?
- In what ways have parents been supported in understanding the modern language of mathematics?
- What math games, books, and resources have you or your teachers offered parents?
- What events have you held (in person or virtual) that help parents connect with each other, their children, or the staff about math?
  - What is the average attendance at these events?
  - How do you make the event accessible?
  - What have you done to increase attendance rates?

Reflect

	Ways We Inform Parents About the Mathematics
What I do or have done	
What others do or have done	

Reflect icon source: Vladislav Popov/iStock.com.

Take a moment and think about things that might be missing from your list. Refer back to the guiding questions we asked you before to see if you can identify gaps or holes in your offerings or communications to parents. Are there events you or your colleagues could have hosted, but didn't? Are there other modes of communication that you or your colleagues have yet to attempt? Are *all* parents included? If not, how can you be sure that *all* parents have equitable access to this critical information?

In reflecting, you might have come up with some ideas of ways in which you or your colleagues could improve in your outreach to parents. Use the following space to jot down any ideas that have come to mind on what you or your colleagues can do more of or differently.

Reflect

	How We Can Better Inform Parents About the Mathematics
What I can do	
What others can do	

Keep your list handy, as you can return to this chart when you are done reading this book and add to it any other ideas that are sparked as a result of reading.

Reflect icon source: Vladislav Popov/iStock.com.

WHAT IS A PARENT'S ROLE IN THEIR CHILD'S MATHEMATICS LEARNING?

The role of a parent is vast and critical in a child's mathematical learning. Despite knowing the importance, we have found that many parents do not feel their schools or districts have adequately explained exactly *what* their role should be. What exactly do schools *want* from parents? How do we convey that to parents? And how do we include parent voices in determining their role?

Many parents have told us they feel like they need to play the role of teacher when supporting their children with mathematics at home. They see their children struggling, specifically in math, and don't know what else to do. Yet when we reflect on what school leaders and educators have told us they actually want, having parents assume the role of a teacher is not it. Other parents see their role as the disciplinarian—the homework authoritarian who forces basic fact memorization through flashcards and drill and kill. These parents mean well and many say they are doing what the school has asked (i.e., supporting basic fact fluency at home), but that is also not the ideal role of a parent. As you will see in Chapter 3, there are several other ways parents view their roles at home. Ultimately, we believe that parents should play the role of coach or mentor, not teacher.

A coach is positive, enthusiastic, supportive, trusting, focused, goal oriented, knowledgeable, observant, respectful, and patient. Our role as educators is to partner with parents to help them exude these qualities when they are supporting their children with mathematics. To do this, we must provide parents with resources and opportunities to develop these skills so they can feel confident in *coaching* their child to mathematical success. This will only strengthen and help to repair much of the current disconnect between families and schools regarding mathematical instruction.

A parent's role as a "math coach" includes being the child's motivator and role model. Parents should maintain a lifelong learning attitude and help their child see that math is everywhere and that everyone can learn to be a mathematical thinker. They should also help their child see that adults use math in everyday life, which makes studying and learning it worthwhile. If available, parents should monitor their child by watching for signs of frustration and providing guidance, not answers. If they are unavailable for that level of support, parents should set up expectations for their child about how to handle frustration and what to do when they do not understand a math assignment. Overall, parents should keep a positive mindset around school and math and encourage their youngster to persevere through challenges.

HOW TO USE THIS BOOK

This book is meant to help you reflect on your current practices and then identify new approaches you could take to improve your work with parents with regard to mathematics education. It includes excerpts from interviews we have conducted with administrators, teachers, curriculum coordinators, and parents to be able to learn from others who have found successful ways to involve families in better understanding 21st century mathematics instruction.

Some parts of the book may be more helpful than others given your particular context. What may work well in a suburban school might not apply in an urban or rural setting, and vice versa. We acknowledge that there are no one-size-fits-all solutions, but you may find ideas you can adapt to your setting.

This book is meant to be useful, applicable, and immediately relevant within whatever context you work. We hope to get your "wheels turning" and inspire you to try something new or find a way to provide more accessibility to what you're already doing. Whatever you can take from this book, we hope you share it. Feel free to dog-ear or mark up the pages or sticky note and tab the book.

This is your resource.

THE GOALS AND STRUCTURE OF THIS BOOK

The goals of this book are to:

- **Comprehend** the parent perspective with regard to their child's mathematics learning,
- **Understand** *what* to communicate mathematically,
- **Explore** *how* to communicate mathematically, and
- **Learn** how to shift the current parent mathematics narrative.

When we engage in conversations with district administrators and teachers about how to work with parents, we often find ourselves discussing many of the same themes. The chapters in this book are based on the frequently asked questions we receive. For your convenience, we now provide a short annotation of each chapter.

 ### Chapter 1: Stepping Into Parents' Shoes

Before we can offer suggestions, we must acknowledge the problem. This chapter highlights exactly what the issues are and helps you see from a varying perspective how many parents feel. As educators, we are biased in that we live and breathe educational jargon and know (or are beginning to know) elementary mathematics content well. Even if we are parents ourselves, our lens is still tainted. This chapter helps us step into the parents' shoes and see the world from their point of view.

 ### Chapter 2: Understanding *What* Parents Need to Know About Today's Math

This chapter focuses on what exactly parents both want and need to know about the shifts in mathematics education. Here, we build on our book, *Adding Parents to the Equation: Understanding Your Child's Elementary School Math* (2019), and discuss how our globalized society has caused a need to shift our instruction. In addition, we discuss *what* parents want and need to know. We also offer our top three facts parents need to know that you might find helpful to communicate with them at the beginning of the year.

 ### Chapter 3: Planning Effective Schoolwide Mathematics Communication

In this chapter, we walk through important schoolwide structures that need to exist, and function, in order to reach *all* parents. You will reflect on the roles and responsibilities of all stakeholders and then consider what must be in place to ensure consistent messaging around homework and report cards. We also provide tips for teachers who work in schools that have not yet achieved schoolwide agreement.

Chapter 4: Exploring *How* to Communicate With Parents About Math

Communication is key—if we do it right. How do you know that what you communicate is done in a way that a parent can and will receive it? What tools or modes of communication do you use? How streamlined is the communication parents receive at both the classroom and school levels? This chapter focuses on how to make your communication more effective and what tools you can use to support communication.

 ## Chapter 5: Exploring *What* to Communicate to Parents About Math

Knowing *how* to communicate with parents will help as you decide *what* to communicate. In this chapter, we look at three levels of communication—schoolwide, classwide, and individual—and offer examples of how at each of these levels you can communicate with parents about mathematics.

 ## Chapter 6: Hosting Parent Events

Part of communicating is offering learning opportunities for parents, too. In this chapter, we will explore various ways to engage parents in their own learning both within and outside of the constructs of the school day. You will engage in stories from the field to learn from other teachers and school leaders about what has worked for them.

Conclusion: Shifting the Narrative

How will you apply and use what you have learned in this book to empower parents and change the paradigm? How will engaging with parents more productively help you? This chapter will allow you a space to reflect and think about how to best use and apply what you have learned throughout this book. We end the book with insights from the field—advice, suggestions, and lessons learned.

Chapter 4 icon source: Momento Design/iStock.com; *Chapter 5 icon source:* Momento Design/iStock.com; *Chapter 6 icon source:* Enis Aksoy/iStock.com.

APPLY IT! TEACHER ACTIVITIES

Look back at the Table of Contents and pick one area of focus that you believe will be most impactful on your practice. As you read, we encourage you to identify ideas and strategies that resonate with you and then set a priority list for implementation. To help you prioritize your efforts, consider the following questions:

1. Why are you reading this book? What do you hope to learn about?

2. What is one thing you wish to convey to parents?

3. What is one way parents could support their children at home that you would find helpful?

4. Think of all the ways that you currently communicate with parents. Are your current methods effective? How do you know?

 Available for download at **resources.corwin.com/partneringwithparents/ elementary**

APPLY IT! SCHOOL LEADER ACTIVITIES

We advise you to first look at the Apply It! Teacher Activities feature and reflect on your purpose for reading this book before thinking about how you can lead change in your school about parental involvement in mathematics. Once you have reflected, consider making it a school initiative to focus on parental involvement. To do this, in the beginning of the year, host a staff meeting where you have staff both reflect on their current practices for involving parents in better understanding math as it's taught today and discuss ways in which all stakeholders in the school could be better at actively involving families in this matter. Here's how it could look:

(continued)

(continued)

1. State the goals and objectives of the meeting.

2. Ask staff to reflect on what they currently do to help parents better understand the way in which we teach math today. Provide sticky notes so staff can write one idea on each note. Consider using the guiding questions from this chapter as the reflection questions.

3. Post chart paper around the room with various headings, such as **Written Communication, In-Person Communication, Digital Communication, Events**, and any other general category. Make sure the headings are very general and broad, so as to capture anticipated responses within the topic.

4. Ask staff to place their sticky notes under the most closely aligned heading.

5. Step back and look as a faculty. Use the following guiding questions for support.

   GUIDING QUESTIONS

   a. What are we doing well? How can we improve what we already do well?

   b. Which area or category is lacking? What is the cause?

   c. What is missing that should be there?

   d. Which areas can we improve?

   e. What is holding us back?

   f. What obstacles are in our way? How do we remove them or work around or through them?

6. Choose one of those broad headings as your initial starting ground for improving family engagement around math.

 Available for download at **resources.corwin.com/partneringwithparents/ elementary**

CHAPTER 1

Stepping Into Parents' Shoes

Tell me and I forget; show me and I may remember; involve me and I understand.

— Chinese Proverb

> "I hate the new math."

> "Why are they changing math?"

> "I just have my child do it my way because it's way faster than all the complicated steps he's being taught to do."

> "It's like I have to learn math all over again."

> "I can't help my kid with her homework."

These quotes from parents might sound familiar to you. Perhaps you have heard some just like these. If not, just peer at the comments

Icon source: Enis Aksoy/iStock.com.

section of any article online that has been tagged with "Common Core" or "new math" and you will surely see responses similar to these. The majority of parents of elementary school children across the nation (especially those who aren't also educators) have major misunderstandings about *what* has changed over time and *why* the change has occurred in the first place. As educators, we must shift the paradigm so parents are more informed and better equipped to support their children at home. In order to do this, we must step into their shoes and try to understand how they feel.

ASKING PARENTS ABOUT SCHOOL COMMUNICATION

Take a moment to imagine a store that you frequent, such as a supermarket or auto store. Now imagine one day you walk in and the aisles are completely turned upside down—what was once in aisle 1 is now somewhere else. How would you feel? What might your reactions be? Write some words in the space provided or draw a picture of your reactions and feelings to this scenario.

Reflect

Reflect icon source: Vladislav Popov/iStock.com.

This very experience might have actually happened to you. Even if it hasn't, you most certainly can relate. Change is challenging for most people, especially without notification. Generally, when we shop for things like groceries or run other similar errands, we want to be efficient. In and out. Quick. Usually that is possible if you find yourself going to the same store often—you've learned the layout, you know exactly where to go. You've built a routine. It's predictable.

If the store's setup has been completely altered, you might find yourself surprised and possibly frustrated. You may feel disoriented as now your task takes more time—it is not as easy as it was before. Perhaps you even take it personally! You might even be so frustrated that you decide to take your business elsewhere.

It might not make sense to you why the change was necessary in the first place, because it was working for you just fine. This is how many parents feel about the shifts in elementary math education. It feels disorienting, sudden, unnecessary, and thus frustrating. Many parents want mathematics to be predictable so they know how to assist their child. The good news? All of this can be changed with proper communication. It's now up to you to be the change agent you always wanted to be!

> "Why would they change the layout? It was working just fine for me!"

Let's dive a bit deeper to better understand how parents feel. Over the past 4 years, we have interviewed over 300 parents of elementary-aged children from more than 15 different states in the United States and three provinces in Canada and asked them to tell us about their experiences with math and school today. Parents represented a variety of settings (rural, suburban, urban, northeast, southeast, east, west) and states that have adopted the Common Core State Standards (or some form of them) and states that have not. We asked them to share with us what their school has done to inform them about the changes, to describe what looks different to them about the math, to elaborate on their excitement and/ or frustration, and more to help us better understand the parent perspective.

Here are some examples of a few of the most popular and powerful sentiments parents felt.

WHAT LOOKS DIFFERENT TO YOU ABOUT YOUR CHILD'S MATH?

The blocks. They start using the visual thing. Ten blocks. I don't really know how to describe it! And word problems! We used to just find the answer. Now they want us to describe how we got to a certain number but it's something simple. And I'm like, "I don't even know what you mean 'describe how you got to this.'"

—Parent of a First Grader

We used to use the words "all you have to do is . . ." or "just do this" . . . but now that doesn't cut it.

—Parent of a Kindergartner and a Fourth Grader

I'd say that it's definitely breaking it down trying to understand why a process is completed vs. just completing it. When I was in school it was all about memorization, just get your times tables down and use that to do the bigger numbers, whereas now they're learning partial products and adding up the values which is helping them understand where that final answer has come from and how he's gotten to that final answer.

—Parent of a Fifth Grader

A lot! So much! When I was going through elementary math in the 80s, I recall a lot of it was related to cartoons—so Pacman ate the . . . you know, the big mouth open eats the small numbers, we had a lot of analogies like that growing up. They're doing things that I have to look up on YouTube to find out. That's not good. Terminology that I don't recognize.

—Parent of First and Fourth Graders

Everything is screen-based for student practice. Thank God he has a teacher this year who sends home worksheets so we have a little idea as to how he's being taught. I can't reinforce what I don't know any information behind! In math, is it the right answer vs. how did we come up with the answer? If I use this method, does it really matter if you use that method if we come to the same conclusion?

—Parent of a Second Grader

I remember having rote memorization things, like times tables and addition and subtraction . . . I remember having flashcards and just memorizing it.

—Parent of a First Grader

I think the biggest difference is that now they're teaching them like what seems 86 different ways to solve a problem and we learned one way . . . it's not the way I know . . . so when he comes home with a paper and I'm like, "I wouldn't even know how to attempt what you just did . . . this is the way that I learned." What they are taught isn't the first thing parents were taught, so there's this like automatic setback to be helpful when they learn new things until they may learn the strategy that we're most familiar with.

—Parent of Third and Fifth Graders

It's the steps that they're told to take. I understand they're getting to the same answers; but it seems like so many more steps than what we're used to.

—Parent of Fourth and Fifth Graders

WHAT HAS BEEN THE MOST EXCITING WITH REGARD TO THE MATH YOUR CHILD IS LEARNING, IF ANYTHING?

It's not just about memorization anymore. It's okay to solve it differently because the focus is on problem-solving. I always thought I was not good at math, yet I realize now that I wasn't good at memorizing—I'd panic and shut down.

—Parent of Third and Sixth Graders

Math is more fun now. From what I've heard from friends who are teachers, it sounds like if we had learned that way, it would have been an easier way to learn, right?

—Parent of a First Grader

I love our kids' math these days! I know many people have issues with it but the approach framing how to solve a problem I think is amazing— you can group by tens or write a number sentence or write fractions in all these different ways. The approach to having a variety of strategies, like having a toolbox that your child can pull from if they need. It speaks to kids who have all these different learning styles.

—Parent of Second and Fifth Graders

Just in general, my kids are learning and coming home with new things, and they are excited about their learning. They seem really confident. It's a great feeling when they come home and they are excited!

—Parent of Third and Fifth Graders

How excited she is! I love that she's so into math; I never was. I feel like having these new methods is helping her be excited about it! I dreaded math, so I'm just happy that she's enjoying it and it's not like a chore—doesn't feel like work to her I think.

—Parent of a First Grader

I like watching him go through it, because it is a subject that jives with him. Seeing him excited to learn these things and him excited to talk about these things is exciting for me.

—Parent of a Second Grader

(Continued)

(Continued)

It's more real world and tangible—not "how does this ever help me in life?" Shows how math is necessary in your life every day.

—Parent of a Third Grader

I love that she gets it! She seems to get it easily. She'll be asking for math problems on the way to baseball. Like clearly some of these strategies are working for her and it's resonating for her.

—Parent of a Second Grader

I definitely see a deeper understanding, even from when I was younger. I feel like it was such a surface-level understanding of just get to the answer, and now he not only wants to get to the answer, but he wants to know the why. And he's more able to catch mistakes with different problems. He is able to go back and locate "oh this is where I went wrong," which is really cool to see.

—Parent of a Fifth Grader

WHAT HAS BEEN THE MOST FRUSTRATING WITH REGARD TO THE MATH YOUR CHILD IS LEARNING, IF ANYTHING?

I don't like having to explain answers that come easy, I guess. I don't see the merit in explaining something simple if you know what the answer is.

—Parent of a First Grader

Not actually knowing what they're [the child] doing.

—Parent of a Kindergartner

How much time it all takes. We used to have sheets of problems. You added or subtracted. That was it. Now she has to draw out a chart with ones, tens, hundreds. It sucks watching her spend 5 minutes doing a problem that should only take 30 seconds.

—Parent of a Second Grader

I think the curriculum calls it a bar model but the teacher was referring to it as a tape model . . . it's [the language] particularly confusing.

—Parent of Third and Sixth Graders

I don't want to undo what he's learned in school, so I have to try [to] figure out what he's doing and the frustration of trying to find that method . . . and even when you look it up [online] it's really difficult to pinpoint it because what his teacher might do with dots and arrays somebody else is doing with boxes, so that is the biggest challenge . . . is trying to match my help with what he's learning in school and there not being any communication to bridge that gap.

—Parent of a Fifth Grader

There's very limited information that comes home. She comes home with a worksheet and there's one example, and I'm trying to follow the work they're showing you, but I don't understand how they're going from Point A to Point B the way they want you to. I don't have any other information to look at to help other than the little problem at the top of the worksheet.

—Parent of a Second Grader

I'm not sure how the math was taught and I don't want to introduce a new way of learning it. I'd rather kinda reinforce the way the teacher is doing it, as opposed to teaching it my way. I don't want to confuse my kid, but I end up having to do it my way or how YouTube does it because I don't know how it's being taught. I have my Master's degree, I have all these certifications, but I cannot remember all these math concepts and don't understand how they're teaching it. How do parents do it when they don't speak the language?

—Parent of First and Fourth Graders

Not getting past my frustration of why they changed math. Can you just answer that question for me?

—Parent of Fourth and Fifth Graders

I don't have a frustration with how he's learning it per se. I think the frustration is more on my part. I can't help him quickly. It's an investment of my time. He may actually understand it better than I do . . . so if he's stuck in something, it's going to take me even longer to be able to help him!

—Parent of a Third Grader

WHAT DO YOU WISH YOUR TEACHERS WOULD DO DIFFERENTLY?

Why are they doing it this way? Short summary on *why* we are learning this way or progression as opposed to saying what the homework is or what topic we are covering. I'm not the expert. If you can help me out a little, that'd be great. Additional resources for parents to try the math [themselves]. I feel like if I am learning while I'm helping with her homework, then I end up doing her homework and I don't want to do that.

—Parent of First and Fourth Graders

More frequent communication . . . What's the progress? Where should their understanding be? How can I help improve that understanding?

—Parent of a Fifth Grader

Send more emails with more details. Tell me what I need to know! Just this conversation alone has been so helpful. It's more than I received from the school.

—Parent of Fourth and Fifth Graders

(Continued)

(*Continued*)

> Can they make a parent companion guide that comes with textbooks? What to do when your child can't answer the question . . . or this is the week they are learning this . . . or a glossary.
>
> —Parent of a Third Grader

> At the beginning of the year, give me a schedule of topics and [say] this is how we teach them, if you'd like to have a parent conference to talk about the methods, that would be really great. If I know how he's supposed to be doing it, I can support.
>
> —Parent of a Second Grader

> Help us understand how this is building our students to be better math learners in maybe a way we weren't doing 25 to 30 years ago. When you reflect back on your experience as a student, you wonder, "I got along just fine . . . I went to college, I have a graduate degree . . . I'm a perfectly capable society member. Why are we doing things so dramatically different?" If there's a real reason, then I think it's important to share. Whether that's a video, a presentation at curriculum night, a handout?
>
> —Parent of Third and Fifth Graders

> Instead of saying kids need to know facts . . . give me something targeted. For example, tell me my kid needs to work on their 6 and 7 facts. Be specific. When people are told to do everything, they shut down.
>
> —Parent of Third and Sixth Graders

As you can see from a small sample set, parents have a lot to say! And what they have to say is meaningful and informative for educators. Their words are formative data for us. We can use their understandings or misunderstandings to help us improve our communication, both the *what* and the *how*, and to appreciate their perspective in a different way. We can also use their positive noticings to continue to build on our strengths.

Reflect

- How did you feel as you read the parents' quotes?

_____

_____

_____

Reflect icon source: Vladislav Popov/iStock.com.

- Which parents' quotes resonated most with you? Why?

  _____

  _____

  _____

- Which parents' quotes are similar to those which you have heard yourself?

  _____

  _____

  _____

- Why do you think parents feel the way they do?

  _____

  _____

  _____

- Think about your own learning experience. What is different in your mathematics teaching or your teachers' mathematics teaching from the way you learned math when you were in elementary school?

  _____

  _____

  _____

WHAT PARENTS DO AND WHY

It is critical to remember that parents want to help their child succeed. As you read in the quotes, some parents have come to embrace the way we teach math—even if they don't fully understand it themselves. Some see their children's excitement and derive their own excitement from it. But far more commonly, parents are frustrated and confused. For those not equipped with an understanding of today's methods and who maybe have not yet come to appreciate the importance of productive struggle, they often want to "rescue" their children. Many parents therefore end up doing at least one of two things:

1. Hindering their child's conceptual development by instructing them in the shortcut methods reflecting how *they* learned the math, sometimes incorrectly; and/or
2. Modeling a negative mindset for their children when they talk about how much they loathe and cannot do the "new" math.

In a 2018 article titled "Just Teach My Kid the <adjective> Math," Dr. James Tanton states that "algorithms are the *definition* of mathematics for so many folk of the past. To not perform these procedures is to not do math." He continues by discussing that the "new" math threatens the use of procedural algorithms with which most parents feel very comfortable because those algorithms summarize most of their learning experiences—they have memories of a rote, step-by-step procedure, which looks nothing like their own children's experiences.

In writing our book *Adding Parents to the Equation: Understanding Your Child's Elementary School Math* (2019), we asked over 200 parents in an informal survey how they feel when their children come home with math today. We found that there were four words that were used most frequently: *intimidated*, *frustrated*, *worried*, and *confused* (Figure 1.1).

Figure 1.1 How Parents Feel About Today's Math

How Parents Feel	Explanation
Intimidated	Because their children are learning math in a totally different way, parents don't believe they can be helpful.
Frustrated	Parents feel unintelligent when unable to do "third-grade math homework."
Worried	Parents are anxious that their children will fail because of them.
Confused	Because parents rarely see anything familiar, math feels like a foreign language.

Source: Kreisberg, H., & Beyranevand, M. L. (2019). *Adding parents to the equation: Understanding your child's elementary school math.* Lanham, MD: Rowman & Littlefield. All rights reserved. Reprinted with permission.

> When parents hinder their children's conceptual development by teaching their children the way they learned or when they complain about the way math is taught today, what we really see is a defense mechanism.

In addition to feeling intimidated, frustrated, worried, and confused, parents also report feeling that reform is a threat to their intelligence and way of knowing. When parents hinder their children's conceptual development by teaching their children the way they learned or when they complain about the way math is taught today, what we really see is a defense mechanism. They are defensive against all of these uncomfortable feelings. They are defensive because they do not yet understand the way we teach math today (the *what*), or what the importance of conceptual understanding is (the *why*), and they aren't yet armed with the proper resources (the *how*).

Parents talked about feeling intimidated because they don't understand the math enough to be helpful. They also described feeling frustrated because elementary math is suddenly beyond their grasp. In addition, parents reported feeling worried that their children would fail because of them. Lastly, parents stated they are confused and feel as if they are speaking a different language than their kids.

What Can We Learn?

This information is powerful. As we looked closer at what the parents were saying, we tried to identify similarities among the responses. If we rewrite some of these generalizations from a parent's perspective, it might look something like this:

- I am intimidated because I can't help my own kid.
- I am frustrated because I feel like my intelligence is under attack.
- I am worried that my child will fail at math because of me.
- I am confused because I didn't learn math this way and there are words, tools, and strategies I don't know.

What we came to realize is that all of these responses were about the parents themselves, not about the kids. Let's look again at these generalizations of a parent's perspective, this time highlighted.

- I am intimidated because I can't help **my** own kid.
- I am frustrated because I feel like **my** intelligence is under attack.
- I am worried that my child will fail at math because of **me**.
- I am confused because **I** didn't learn math this way and there are words, tools, and strategies **I don't know**.

It has been said that one's ego is indirectly proportional to one's level of knowledge. Albert Einstein said it best when he stated, "the more the knowledge, the lesser the ego; the lesser the knowledge, the more the ego." Right now, parents' egos are heightened because their knowledge is being threatened. They are feeling unintelligent and helpless. It's our job as educators to repair how they see and view *themselves* in relation to mathematics and give them the information and tools they need to be empowered as partners. Because, as much as this is about their children, it's really **about them**.

Let's go back to the parent responses and see if we can tell what the parents *didn't* say. When we read between the lines and rewrite those generalizations again, but this time focusing on what parents actually want, we are able to make sense of their needs differently.

- I want to be able to help my own kid.
- I want to feel intelligent, especially in front of my child.
- I want to feel confident that my child will succeed.
- I want to be able to talk with my child about the math they are learning.

At the end of the day, parents just want to feel **helpful**, **intelligent**, **confident**, and **familiar** with the language.

Four Core Wants

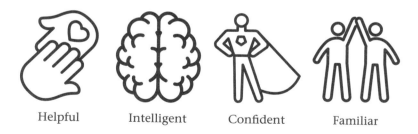

Helpful   Intelligent   Confident   Familiar

We contend that if we as an educational community help parents and families achieve these "four core wants," then families will feel at ease again and will also help us to empower parents as partners to help further the math learning goals we have for our students.

Four core wants icon sources: Helpful by appleuzr/iStock.com; Intelligent by PeterSnow/ iStock.com; Confident by Bigmouse108/iStock.com; Familiar by PeterSnow/iStock.com.

PUTTING IT ALL TOGETHER

In this chapter, you stepped into parents' shoes to understand their perspective, how they feel about the way we teach mathematics today, and why they feel the way they do. We have to be aware of the parent perspective to be able to acknowledge their desires. Then, we can empower parents because they are the ones who have the greatest influence on the children we teach. The first way we suggest doing this is by helping parents understand the *why* and the *what*, which we will talk about in Chapter 2.

 FREQUENTLY ASKED QUESTIONS

Q **How do I respond to a parent who says, "I learned math by memorizing facts and formulas and I turned out just fine."**

A This is true that this approach worked for some people, but it did not work for all. The way we teach math today helps more students understand, recall, and apply the mathematics that they learn. In addition, as our world globalizes, we must adapt the way we teach mathematics to promote the skills needed for students to be successful in their future careers using new technology.

Q **I notice in this chapter that there are some positive statements from parents. Were those statements from parents who also shared frustrations?**

A Yes. In our interview process, we only came across one parent (who does not play the dual role of educator *and* parent) who *exclusively* spoke positively about the math we teach today and how their school has handled the shifts in instruction and communication to parents. But it's also important to note that while that parent was not an educator, they were the vice president of the school's parent teacher organization and self-identified as strong in mathematics.

APPLY IT! TEACHER ACTIVITIES

How Will You Use Parent Perspectives to Inform Your Decisions?

Though we have spent years interviewing parents, their experiences are not always generalizable. It is critical that you spend time getting to know your students' caregivers in order to provide your students the most effective instruction. Remember, when your students go home, their "first" teachers, their guardians, have to be on board with what we are doing in schools to be able to foster a positive mindset and support the learning. One of the best ways to do that is to send home a survey or questionnaire that truly allows you to step into the parents' shoes and understand their perspective.

Feel free to use our survey or create your own. We suggest sending this survey home at the beginning of the year so you can gather as much data as possible around current mindsets about math among your students' families, caregivers' personal experiences around math, and more. We want you to make this as personalized as possible. Add questions that feel more relevant to your context. If you want to specify the survey for your particular grade level, feel free to add specific questions about strategies or vocabulary parents will see this school year. Send the survey home digitally and/or via hard copy, and be sure to have the survey translated into the native languages of your students' guardians by reaching out to your translation/bilingual departments or campus administration. For more information on how and when to use this survey, see Chapter 5.

Grades PreK–5 Beginning of the Year Survey

Dear Families,

In an effort to provide your child the best math experience, I am asking you to take 5–10 minutes to complete a survey. This survey will help me better understand how I can support your child's learning of mathematics this year. This is a wonderful opportunity to ask questions you have about how math is taught today so that I can best support you, as well. Please take a moment to answer the following questions as best as you can.

Apply It! icon source: PeterSnow/iStock.com.

About YOU

1   The following describes your school life *when you were a child*. (Select all that apply.)

☐   I received formal schooling in the United States.

☐   I received formal schooling outside of the United States.

☐   I was homeschooled.

☐   I did not receive formal schooling.

☐   I prefer not to say.

2   The following best describes your attitude toward math *when you were a child*. (Choose one.)

☐   Loved it!

☐   Liked it.

☐   Didn't love it, but didn't hate it.

☐   Hated it!

☐   Can't remember.

Comments (if any):

3   The following best describes your attitude toward math *now as an adult*. (Choose one.)

☐   Love it!

☐   Like it.

☐   Don't love it, but don't hate it.

☐   Hate it!

(*Continued*)

(*Continued*)

If there was a change, what caused it?

4   Check all the statements that are *true* for you.

☐   I feel familiar and confident with the way math is taught today.

☐   I am excited to learn new ways of looking at and thinking about math.

☐   I am nervous I will confuse my child if I try to help them.

☐   I don't understand how math is being taught today.

☐   I don't understand why math is being taught differently than the way I learned it.

About YOUR CHILD

I   The following best describes *your child's* attitude toward math. (Choose one.)

☐   Loves it!

☐   Likes it.

☐   Doesn't love it, but doesn't hate it.

☐   Hates it!

☐   I don't know because they never talk about it.

Comments (if any):

2 How do you support your child's understanding of math? (Check all that apply.)

- [ ] I read books about math with my child often.

- [ ] We play games and puzzles that involve math.

- [ ] We do flashcards and help them memorize their facts by repetition.

- [ ] We do fact review but through games.

- [ ] I ask my child to show and explain to me what they learn each day.

- [ ] We find math in everyday life and talk about it.

- [ ] I help them with their homework.

- [ ] Other: _____

3 What information do you feel you need about the math your child will learn this year?

4 What else do you think I should know that will help me understand how to support you and your child's math learning this year?

APPLY IT! SCHOOL LEADER ACTIVITIES

How Will You Use Parent Perspectives to Inform Your Decisions?

Consider working with teachers to send the Beginning of the Year Survey (shown in the Teacher Activities feature) home to parents to ensure consistency across grade levels. What action plans can you put into place to help teachers organize the results? How can your school use the results to inform larger school initiatives? How could the data help you get a sense of where the school should go next with parent support in mathematics? *Reminder:* see Chapter 5 for more information on this survey.

Should you choose not to use our suggested survey, what other ways can you . . .

- "Step into parents' shoes" in your school or district to gain a deeper sense of where parents are in their understanding of today's mathematics?

- Collaborate with teachers to determine which events are essential to host this year?

- Discuss with teachers which types of communication are "must-dos" as a result of what you learn about your particular parents' needs mathematically?

 Available for download at **resources.corwin.com/partneringwithparents/ elementary**

CHAPTER 2

Understanding *What* Parents Need to Know About Today's Math

Parents are products of the old education, and therefore they define mathematics as the skills they were taught. When they don't see their children learning what they believe to be the goals of mathematics—the algorithms—they assume that nothing is being learned.

—Cathy Fosnot and Maarten Dolk (2001)

Before we jump into ways in which we can support and communicate with parents as our mathematics instruction continues to evolve, we must all be able to articulate why the shift has happened in the first place. In other words, we need to help parents understand the *why* behind the *what* in what they commonly call this "new math." More importantly, we must describe the *what* accurately.

Many parents currently think the *what* is that math has changed suddenly and the *why* is because of the government and testing. They are not wrong to think such things. Think about where they get their information if schools are not providing adequate and

IN THIS CHAPTER YOU WILL . . .

- Determine what parents *really* need to know about *today's* mathematics teaching and learning,
- Examine resources that support communicating about today's math, and
- Identify what parents *really* need to know about their *own* child's math.

Icon source: PeterSnow/iStock.com.

correct rationales: social media, celebrities, movies, the news, and even conversations with other parents play a large role in the misinformation that parents have obtained over the years. Without adequate information from the education community, this misinformation has often created an echo-chamber effect.

As educators, we know that the actual content of mathematics has not changed: 1 + 1 still equals 2 (in the base-ten number system). We also know that the government and testing did not drive the shift in the way we teach math. So, how do we communicate this information to parents? Humans are answer driven and need rationales to explain phenomena. It is up to us educators and leaders to help families understand the *what* and *why*.

What's the bottom line? As most educators have come to understand, the *what* is actually that the pedagogical routines and the way in which we teach have adjusted to be more student centered and inquiry or exploratory based. The *why* is that research has shown that this way of teaching

1. Provides better learning opportunities for *all*, not some;
2. Better reflects what we know from newer brain-based research about the way children developmentally learn; and
3. Prepares our children better for the future.

WHAT PARENTS *REALLY* NEED TO KNOW ABOUT TODAY'S MATH

Not all things are important to communicate. Most parents are not looking to relearn math and we certainly do not need to give them more procedures than they already know. We also do not want parents to take on the role of teacher, as that is our job and often parents teach skills incorrectly that later we must undo. So, what do parents really need to know?

In Chapter 1, we described parents' four core wants. Let's start with what parents *want* to know and build from there.

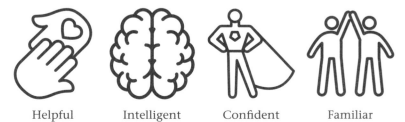

Helpful   Intelligent   Confident   Familiar

Four core wants icon sources: Helpful by appleuzr/iStock.com; Intelligent by PeterSnow/iStock.com; Confident by Bigmouse108/iStock.com; Familiar by PeterSnow/iStock.com.

If parents want to feel **helpful**, **intelligent**, **confident**, and **familiar with the language**, how can we make that happen?

Our Top Three Facts Every Parent Needs to Know About Today's Math

1. Math instruction evolves . . . just like everything else.
2. Mathematics is not a gene.
3. We prepare kids for the future, not today.

First, we can help parents understand that the math they learned is the same math their children are learning, but *how* students today are learning it and *when* is different. It is critical that parents today understand that the way we teach math evolves over time as we learn from newer research, gain more experience, and see how cultural, social, and emotional experiences impact the teaching and learning of math.

Next, we can help reframe parents' mindsets. Most parents grew up during a time when doing well in math was often attributed to speed. As a result, many have used this limited measuring stick to determine that they weren't good at math and perhaps were not born with "a math gene." Many parents operate with a **fixed mindset**, where they believe intelligence is a measured indicator of future success, especially when it comes to mathematics. Over the years, schools have done an incredible job helping students outgrow a *fixed mindset* and shift toward identifying with a **growth mindset**. While many school leaders, educators, and students have adopted new perspectives, it is vital that parents join in this mission, too.

Finally, we must help parents understand that while their children are in school *today*, our goal isn't to prepare children for today—in fact, our goal is to prepare them for their *future*. This means sometimes teaching them skills that will be more applicable later than they are now.

Let's dive deeper into these three topics.

In a **fixed mindset**, people believe their intelligence, personality, and talent are permanent and unchangeable.

In a **growth mindset**, people believe that their intelligence, personality, talent, and other basic abilities are developmental and changeable dependent on effort.

Math Instruction Evolves . . . Just Like Everything Else

As most things do, math instruction evolves over time. Because parents were often raised under the notion that mathematics is a study of procedures, they frequently think about math in a binary way (that it is either right or wrong) and that there is only one way to do it (the right way).

> We cannot continue to teach a core subject in a way that only works for some.

Time and time again we hear parents complain about the way we are currently teaching math, yet they simultaneously boast that they are terrible at math or that they hate math. When we offer parent workshops, this is the first question we ask: "Raise your hand if you hated math, disliked math, or were fearful of math as a kid." Usually, most hands go up. Parents today are generally not seeing the grander picture that many of them fear math themselves and that the way we taught math in the past didn't work for everyone. It didn't prepare many for future careers in mathematics, nor did it prepare us to feel confident and able in the subject. We cannot continue to teach a core subject in a way that only works for some. *This* is what parents need to know.

> Advancements in technology and research have impacted how and what we teach in mathematics.

In addition, teaching is both a science and art. Therefore, we often must adjust our methods to meet the needs of society. As technology has globalized and advanced, the way we teach math must adapt. In the past, you may have justified to students that knowing their math facts was important because they "won't always have a calculator in their back pocket." Well, our kids are laughing at us now! Math facts are readily available at the drop of a "Hey Siri . . ." or "Alexa, . . ." and we can Google anything we want or need to know.

Advancements in technology and research have impacted how and what we teach in mathematics. *This* is also what parents need to know. This is not to say that knowing your multiplication facts fluently isn't important or, better yet, helpful; but it is less critical today than when we were in school. The whole idea is that if we aren't fluent in one skill or topic, then we have other strategies and means of achieving the same result, even if it means doing so in a less efficient manner. Ultimately, we are teaching toward fluency and automaticity in different ways that involve reasoning and logic, so that children can think critically and problem-solve when a quick solution is not readily available.

We have found that the key to helping parents understand this information is by presenting them with relatable analogies. For example, using the evolution of the telephone can be a relatable analogy that we find often helps parents make connections between how mathematics instruction evolves over time. Since many parents own or have seen a cell phone, they can relate. Ensuring your analogies are accessible is critical.

When we start our parent night talks, we often joke and say, "Take a moment and pull out your rotary phone." And parents look at us like we are nuts. Then we say, "What's that? You don't have one? Why not?" Parents tend to call out things like, "We have newer phones! Technology changes! Outdated!" They always answer their own question for themselves! We continue with, "Let's apply your answers now to mathematics instruction. 'Why don't we teach math the same way we used to?' Because technology has advanced and improved—the old way is outdated—and as a result, we have more effective tools and methods."

We often finish our bit with a picture of the evolution of a telephone (similar to Figure 2.1) and say something like, "We are sure Alexander Graham Bell would be rolling over in his grave if he saw that his invention, the telephone, now acts like a computer, television, fax machine, calculator, and more!" This analogy helps parents see that an invention that originally served one purpose can either adapt and evolve to serve other purposes as a result of the changing times or it can become extinct.

Figure 2.1 – Evolution of the Telephone

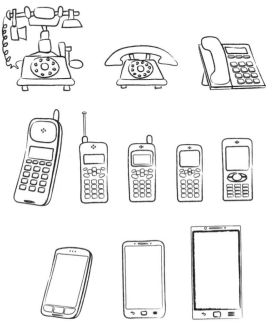

Source: Romanovskyy/iStock.com.

Mathematics instruction is no different. An example can be seen through the evolution of how basic operations are taught. In the past, teachers would often teach algorithms procedurally, showing one step at a time; students would regurgitate the steps on new problems until they'd mastered the procedure. This method, however, did not generally develop students into problem-solvers who can apply understandings in multiple contexts. Therefore, most standards today suggest that teachers reserve more procedural or traditional algorithms until after students have developed a deeper conceptual understanding.

It is important that we communicate with parents that teaching is as much a science as it is an art. As we learn more about how kids learn, and specifically how people best learn mathematics, we adjust how we teach to match. In the words of Adam Welcome, "We can't teach WiFi students with landline strategies."

Let's look at one parent's account of her experience at a parent–teacher conference. During this 5- to 10-minute conversation, the parent had already begun to feel more comfortable with newer mathematics instruction simply by hearing the purpose of the change.

> *Really the most comfortable I have really been has been mid-year when we had our parent–teacher conference and I chatted with her teacher about this. Her teacher gave some me insight into how she is teaching and I was all of a sudden more comfortable with the new way we learn math now . . . but I had to ask the teacher to get this information.*

> *So when I sat down with her teacher, her teacher explained it in a way that I had not heard it before. The whole point is to give them different concepts and tools to understand how to do the same thing but in different ways—so that knowing each kid learns in a different way, maybe one context resonates more with one student than another student. Because I was very confused about how some of these things were working and I wanted to know why we are doing 5,000 different ways to get to the same answer . . . so when she described it like that, I said that makes a ton of sense! So that in my brain [it] clicked and I said I won't be frustrated anymore because now I kinda get where you're going to.*

All it took was the teacher providing a high-level overview of *why* we have changed our methods of instruction for this parent to suddenly feel relieved—and, more importantly, to trust the process and support the work of her child's teacher. This conversation took place mid-year; had this teacher found the opportunity to communicate this information earlier on, perhaps the parent would have felt more at ease and been better equipped to support their child from the beginning.

Mathematics Is Not a Gene

Just as technology and instructional methods evolve over time, so does our understanding. Many adults had poor math experiences growing up, which led them to believe they were not cut out for the subject. Additionally, in the past, many of us experienced that being efficient—getting to the answer quickly while showing the least amount of work—was highly valued. We thought that performing with the least amount of resources, time, and effort equated to a better mathematics student, perhaps even a more intelligent student.

While some research indicates a correlation between speed and intelligence (Sheppard & Vernon, 2008), other research suggests that the pressure to perform quickly can cause misfires in our brain and result in anxiety; this ultimately causes someone to perform poorly in math or develop a fear of the subject in general (Boaler, 2015, 2016). Parents need to see that being fast isn't what makes us smart. When we focus on right versus wrong in mathematics or put a heavy emphasis on the answers to math problems rather than the strategies and processes, students ultimately see mathematics as a subject they can or cannot "do" (Boaler, 2016). We may once have thought we must be born into a mathematical family to be able to do mathematics well, but this thinking has expired. It is critical we communicate that with parents.

Now we realize that anyone can be a mathematician. It turns out that mathematics is not actually a gene we are born with (Boaler, 2016), but rather a subject that we all can grow to understand and love. We have also come to learn that being effective is far more important than being efficient. Being effective means that we accomplish a task, despite any challenges or problems thrown our way. This could mean that we solve it efficiently, too, but it doesn't mean we *have* to do so. When we think about mathematics, no famous mathematician develops theories or proves them quickly. They take their time, adjust their work to be reasonable, and problem-solve. These habits are the emphasis of someone who views themselves as a learner, always growing and developing. We want kids today to exhibit these behaviors as they study mathematics—being thoughtful and intentional and using reasoning skills to solve new and unfamiliar problems. In order for parents to be able to support this mindset at home, they must understand the difference between a *fixed mindset* and a *growth mindset*.

As a reminder, a *fixed mindset* means you believe your intelligence is stagnant (Dweck, 2006). People who ascribe to a fixed mindset believe their intelligence and other basic qualities create success, rather than focusing on the effort needed to attain an accomplishment (Dweck, 2015). In the case of mathematics, having a *fixed mindset* means you believe you are either a "math" person or not. Those who have a *fixed mindset* in math think that math is a gene and that if they were not born predisposed or inclined toward achieving in mathematics, then they are incapable. Parents often operate under a *fixed mindset* with respect to mathematics. They freely (and sometimes proudly) admit to their children that they "were/are bad at math" or "are not a math person."

A *growth mindset* means you believe your intelligence can develop over time and with experience (Dweck, 2006). People who ascribe to a growth mindset believe that success is found by hard work, effort, and resilience and that they can always learn and grow (Dweck, 2015). In the case of mathematics, having a *growth mindset* means you believe there is no such thing as a math gene and you recognize that with effort and perseverance, you can achieve. Many schools today reinforce the ideas of a *growth mindset* through read-alouds, sentence starters displayed on bulletin boards, and conversations. Yet how do we expect children to actually have a *growth mindset* when their role model, and oftentimes the person who gave them their "bad math genes," articulates their inability to solve math problems and fear of math?

Figure 2.2 illustrates how someone with a fixed or growth mindset handles or reacts to challenges, obstacles, effort, criticism, and the success of others and shows the impact of the identified mindset.

Figure 2.2 – Fixed Versus Growth Mindset

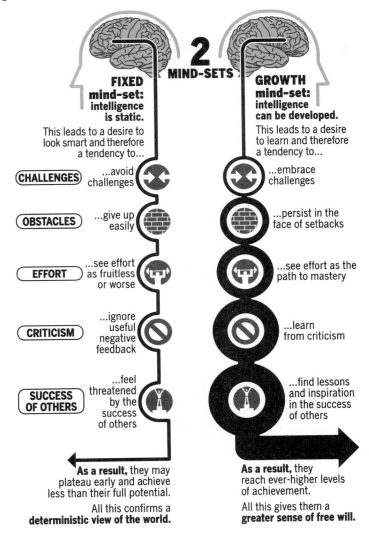

Research shows that parents also have a strong influence on their children's mindset. According to a study conducted by Vitale (2020), 80% of high school students who were tested to showcase a "growth mindset" talked about the impact that their parents had in developing these beliefs. Likewise, students who were tested to showcase a "fixed mindset" also attributed parental influence as a factor for their beliefs. One student stated that her mother sympathized with her because she, too, was 'bad' at math in high school. In addition to this sympathy, the student explained, 'She's not as hard on a math grade as she would be an English grade' (Vitale, 2020, p. 104). This idea of labeling, whether self-imposed or not (e.g., labeling someone or themselves as "bad at math"), impacts people's mindsets about their abilities. Because parents' beliefs and language hold such heavy influence on children, it is vital that we ensure they understand the impacts and alternative ways to communicate in a strengths-based manner at home.

As we continue to work daily preparing our students to foster a growth mindset, we have yet to transform society-at-large around mindsets in mathematics. We recently saw a car with a bumper sticker that proudly boasted, "I can't math." Can you imagine how society would scoff at a car if the bumper sticker read "I can't think" or "I can't read"? As a society, we have deemed it perfectly acceptable to be "bad" at math. We must teach parents that conveying these messages to their children further delays their math learning and often causes them to fear the subject, regardless of their abilities.

To help combat these beliefs, it is important that schools provide parents resources and information about developing their own growth mindset.

> Can you imagine how society would scoff at a car if the bumper sticker read "I can't think" or "I can't read"? As a society, we have deemed it perfectly acceptable to be "bad" at math.

Resources on Growth Mindset

GROWTH MINDSET RESOURCES FOR PARENTS

Books

- *Mindset: The New Psychology of Success* by Carol Dweck (2006)
- *Mathematical Mindsets* by Jo Boaler (2016)
- *Mindsets for Parents: Strategies to Encourage Growth Mindsets in Kids* by Mary Cay Ricci and Margaret Lee (2016)

Video

- "Growth Mindset vs. Fixed Mindset" by John Spencer on YouTube, https://www.youtube.com/watch?v=M1CHPnZfFmU

Websites

- "Growth Mindset for Parents" from MindsetKit, https://www.mindsetkit.org/growth-mindset-parents
- "Parent Resources" from YouCubed, https://www.youcubed.org/resource/parent-resources/

GROWTH MINDSET RESOURCES FOR CHILDREN

Books

- *Everyone Can Learn Math* by Alice Aspinall (2018)
- *When Sophie Thinks She Can't* by Molly Bang (2018)
- *The Girl Who Never Made Mistakes* by Mark Pett and Gary Rubinstein (2011)
- *What Do You Do With a Problem?* by Kobi Yamada (2016)
- *What Do You Do With an Idea?* by Kobi Yamada (2014)
- *Jabari Jumps* by Gaia Cornwall (2019)
- *Mae Among the Stars* by Roda Ahmed (2018)
- *Perfect Ninja: A Children's Book About Developing a Growth Mindset* by Mary Nhin (2019)
- *Hana Hashimoto, Sixth Violin* by Chieri Uegaki (2014)
- *The Book of Mistakes* by Corinna Luyken (2017)
- *Beautiful Oops!* by Barney Saltzberg (2010)

In addition to readings that can help both parents and their children, parents also need support with understanding that their words heavily influence their children. To combat this, school leaders and teachers should provide parents with a reference sheet on what they might be saying at home and what they can say instead to support their child's mathematical development. Use Figure 2.3 to help parents understand that today we want to praise and reward effort and process over results and intelligence, nurture the belief that risk-taking fosters growth (not that it could mean failure), emphasize process and perseverance over answers and outcomes, frame mistakes as part of the learning process rather than as bad habits, and communicate high expectations.

Figure 2.3 – Growth Versus Fixed Mindset Language in Mathematics for Parents

Instead of . . .	Try This
Praising Results and Intelligence • "You got it all correct. You're so smart." • "You even got the hardest one right. Genius!"	**Praise Effort and Process** • "Wow! You did great on that. You must have worked really hard." • "That problem looks tricky. Tell me about how you did it."
Nurturing the Belief That Risk-Taking Could Mean Failure • "If you don't know, just skip it and do the ones you do know."	**Nurture the Belief That Risk-Taking Fosters Growth** • "You took a risk to challenge yourself and you succeeded. That must feel really good." • "You took a risk to challenge yourself and even though you haven't found the answer, you succeeded in being brave. That must feel really good."
Emphasizing Answers and Outcomes • "Check your answer. It's wrong." • "I want you to fix numbers 2, 3, 5, and 7 on your homework. The answers aren't right."	**Emphasize Process and Perseverance** • "I'm proud of you for trying. You can't succeed without an attempt." • "I'm proud of you for sticking to it and not quitting. Regardless of the outcome, you did a great job trying." • "Can you tell me about your process for number 2 on your homework?"
Framing Mistakes as Bad • "You're making sloppy and silly mistakes. You need to pay attention."	**Frame Mistakes as Part of the Learning Process** • "It's important to treat your brain like a muscle. The more you make mistakes, the more you learn."
Rewarding Results • "Nice work! You got all the problems correct. You can have screen time tonight."	**Reward Effort and Process** • "Nice work! You earned screen time tonight because I saw you putting in your best effort on your work. Thanks for trying your best."
Communicating Low Expectations • "Why don't you stick to what you know and are good at?"	**Communicate High Expectations** • "You are capable, which is why I challenge you and hold such high expectations." • "I know you can do this."

Source: Adapted from © 2014 Transforming Education.

In the end, it is vital that parents understand that learning takes time and patience, isn't about swiftness, and doesn't indicate level of intelligence. Rushing to accelerate our children, pushing memorization over deep understanding, and labeling our children as gifted and talented will not create problem-solvers and critical thinkers. Communicating to parents that we teach mathematics to children so they can be successful in their future is of utmost importance.

We Prepare Students for the Future, Not Today

It is also important that we remind parents that our job as math educators is not to teach kids math that they use today—it is to prepare them for the future. We need to anticipate the math that will be useful when kids enter the workforce and teach them the skills necessary to be successful later, not now.

The World Economic Forum's *Future of Jobs Report* (2016, 2018) indicates that complex problem-solving, critical thinking, and creativity are top skills that future job seekers need. By showing parents that world economists, chief executive officers of top-performing businesses, and others agree that math can no longer be taught as an isolated subject of computational skills but rather as an interdisciplinary subject focused on problem-solving with logic, reasoning, and communication skills, we can help parents better understand that these shifts are supported outside and beyond the contexts of traditional schooling. Because we have technology that can do simple tasks for us, workers must now have more advanced thinking that cannot be replaced by automation (such as enhanced communication abilities, problem-solving strategies, and more). Whether students enter a technical career or college-track profession, having these enhanced skills will best prepare them for their future work life.

Developing children to enter a world of problem-solving means we must normalize struggle and teach parents about the habits that promote mathematical thinking. Normalizing struggle means we encourage students to persevere through challenging tasks and we make our struggle visible. Children need to see that things do not always come easy; if we, as educators and parents, can model that for our students and children, then they will begin to own that thinking, too. This will help to cultivate the problem-solving traits that our children need for the future. Unfortunately, far too often parents do not value struggle as a positive mathematics learning trait.

> **Normalizing struggle means we encourage students to persevere through challenging tasks and we make our struggle visible.**

We must help parents understand how to move from unproductive to productive beliefs about struggle. For example, sharing with parents what struggle actually means (such as providing them Figure 2.4) will help them reframe their mindset, if needed.

Figure 2.4 – Normalizing Struggle

Unproductive Beliefs	Productive Beliefs
Children who are good at math don't struggle.	All students should have the opportunity to struggle in math because struggle that results in success allows students to see they can overcome challenges.
Struggle lowers confidence.	Struggle builds confidence. People thrive when they see success after challenge.
Faster is better. Struggle is a signal that one isn't good at math.	Math is not about speed. Struggling means the content is appropriately challenging.

Source: Adapted from SanGiovanni, J. J., Katt, S., & Dykema, K. J. (2020). *Productive math struggle*. Thousand Oaks, CA: Corwin.

Ultimately, normalizing struggle goes back to understanding that math is not a gene and that performing something fast does not equate to being smart. Instead, fostering a growth mindset results in a desire to learn, not a desire to appear intelligent. A desire to learn is quite possibly one of the most powerful traits a human can have. We must normalize struggle to be able to create future problem-solvers who publicly fail and succeed, collaboratively.

In addition to normalizing struggle, parents must also understand the habits that mathematical thinkers exhibit. In many of today's mathematics classrooms, content standards (the mathematics) drive most of our instruction, but it is the practice and process standards (the habits of mathematical thinkers) that create problem-solvers and critical thinkers. Take a look at the popularly used Standards for Mathematical Practice (National Governors Association Center for Best Practices, Council of Chief State School Officers, 2010).

Standards for Mathematical Practice

1. Make sense of problems and persevere in solving them.
2. Reason abstractly and quantitatively.
3. Construct viable arguments and critique the reasoning of others.
4. Model with mathematics.
5. Use appropriate tools strategically.
6. Attend to precision.
7. Look for and make use of structure.
8. Look for and express regularity in repeated reasoning.

Source: National Governors Association Center for Best Practices, Council of Chief State School Officers (2010).

Whether you are familiar with the Standards for Mathematical Practice or another set of process standards, the concept is the same. Practice and process standards focus on skills mathematicians use daily. These habits of mind, such as persevering, reasoning, communicating mathematical ideas, and sense-making, are skills that students will take with them well beyond the mathematical context.

Helping parents understand *how* to foster these skills at home is critical. In Chapter 4, we dive deeply into *how* to communicate and we provide examples of how to embed these skills within your correspondence with parents.

The bottom line is this: the way *we* learned math would not set up our students today for the skills necessary to persevere, problem-solve, and reason in *their* future. We need to help parents see and understand that math instruction evolves just like everything else, that mathematics is not a gene, and that we prepare their children for the future, not for today. We also must recognize that parents want to feel *helpful, intelligent, confident,* and *familiar with the language,* so we must provide them resources and opportunities to achieve those goals. As you continue to read this book, you will find more and more ways to provide parents opportunities to achieve their four core wants.

WHAT PARENTS *REALLY* NEED TO KNOW ABOUT THEIR CHILD'S MATH

In addition to understanding what they *really* need to know about 21st century mathematics in general, parents also need to know some specifics about their child's math each year in order to provide the best support at home. Figure 2.5 describes other important aspects parents must know.

Knowing what parents need to know both about today's math teaching and learning, and about their child's math in particular, is helpful. But knowing what structures need to be in place to support this *and* how to communicate these needs to parents is vital. This will be the in-depth focus of Chapters 3–6.

Figure 2.5 – What Parents Really Need to Know About Their Child's Math

- What their role entails as a child's "math coach," including school and teacher expectations of parent support (covered in Chapter 3)
- What topics their child will be learning at a particular grade level
- What models, representations, and tools their children will be using in class and at home to learn math
- What strategies their child will learn for reference
- Why we are teaching the strategies we are, especially if they are unfamiliar to parents
- How the strategies their child will learn connect to the strategies most adults are familiar with
- How they can foster their child's growth mathematically
- How they can communicate with the teacher regarding their child's math progress
- When they should help their child and when they should not

PUTTING IT ALL TOGETHER

In this chapter, we explored *what* parents really need to know about today's mathematics teaching and learning and, more specifically, what they really need to know about their own child's math learning. In the next few chapters, we will uncover how to communicate these needs to parents.

 FREQUENTLY ASKED QUESTIONS

Q I often hear parents say that they are "not a math person." What are some ways we as educators and school leaders can challenge the "I'm not a math person" social acceptance?

A We have found that the best way to help combat the notion that there is a mathematics gene is to share with parents real-life stories of people who struggled with something yet became successful with practice and effort. For example, you might have a personal story you could share. Alternatively, you might use a celebrity's story to make your point (e.g., Michael Jordan did not make the varsity basketball team his sophomore year of high school). In addition, when you hear another adult speak negatively about the "new math" or boast about their inability to do math, challenge them. The only way to change the narrative is to bring attention and self-awareness to it. Dig deep into how and why they feel the way they do and educate them as to the repercussions of making those comments in front of their children.

Q **I am struggling to change some parents' mindsets. Can you share an experience where you have successfully altered a parent's mindset?**

A There was one family that Matthew encountered who did not follow any of the general recommendations he offered, some of which were described in this chapter. Eventually, he asked the parents to make a deal with him. He said if they made *one* change for a few weeks and it had no impact on their daughter, then he would never bother them again with the recommendations. They agreed. He asked them to shift the way they praised their child. Instead of focusing on results, he asked them to praise her effort. Not surprisingly, after 4 weeks, the child's perception around her perceived mathematics ability started to shift and the parents were more open to learning other strategies to continue the positive shift they had seen in their daughter.

Q **Why do we have a difficult time allowing ourselves to evolve with the changes to math instruction?**

A Aside from the notion that humans in general struggle with change, there are a couple of reasons we believe people have a difficult time accepting the changes to math instruction. First, everyone has an opinion about how math instruction *should* be done, mainly because most of the folks with an opinion went to school and experienced math themselves. Because of this, most people equate familiarity with understanding. Just because you have experience with something does not make you an expert. Second, many people are fearful that the change might expose their lack of understanding, which then puts them in a precarious situation if they are to help their children.

APPLY IT! TEACHER ACTIVITIES

How Will You Help Parents Understand What They Need to Know?

☐ What events or correspondence do you plan or send out at the classroom level that can impact how parents understand today's math?

In Chapter 4, you will read about *how* to write to parents about math. Take some time before reading ahead to apply what you read in this chapter by writing or examining your current, beginning of year letter to parents. What would you include based on what you read in this chapter?

APPLY IT! SCHOOL LEADER ACTIVITIES

How Will You Help Parents Understand What They Need to Know?

☐ What events or correspondence do you plan or send out at the school level that can impact how parents understand today's math?

In Chapter 3, you will read about schoolwide structures that impact parent involvement in math. Take some time before reading ahead to think about the roles and responsibilities of all stakeholders in your school. Whose role is it to communicate to parents about what they need to know from this chapter?

CHAPTER 3

Planning Effective Schoolwide Mathematics Communication

Every system is perfectly designed to get the results it gets.
— Donald Berwick

Teachers, administrators, and staff all play critical roles in educating our students, yet parents arguably play the most important role. Consider this analogy: to keep a strong and beautiful flowering plant healthy, one must attend to all of its parts—flowers, roots, and leaves and stem. Imagine students represent the blossoming flowers, parents are the roots, and educators and staff, curriculum, and professional development make up the leaves and stem. Schools readily water the flowers, leaves, and stem; yet if they don't attend to the roots as closely, the once-flowering plant will begin to wilt. Having clearly defined schoolwide structures will have positive impacts on parent communication around mathematics, much like attending to all parts of the plant will prevent the flower from wilting.

IN THIS CHAPTER YOU WILL . . .

- Reflect on various stakeholders' roles and responsibilities in elementary mathematics teaching and learning,
- Recognize the importance of crafting clear and consistent messaging around homework and report cards and how a lack of consistency can impact parent understanding of mathematics, and
- Consider commitments you can make toward addressing parents' mathematics needs within your own control and as a school community.

Icon source: rambo182/iStock.com.

THE SYSTEMIC PROBLEM

System: A set of things or people that work together to operate.

. . . .

The problem is clear: our education system has not provided parents the much needed resources and tools to navigate the changes that have occurred.

. . . .

Schools and districts are systems. If a **system** is defined as a set of things or people that work together to operate, then in schools the system focuses primarily on the people most visible inside the rhetorical building (students, teachers, staff, leaders, even policy-makers) and often unwittingly puts the people outside the building (parents, families, and other community members) on the back burner. As we saw in Chapter 1, many parents feel out of the loop, which leaves them feeling intimidated, frustrated, worried, and confused. The problem is clear: our education system has not provided parents the much needed resources and tools to navigate the changes that have occurred.

As we noted in Chapter 1, we interviewed parents from various regions of the United States and Canada who voluntarily signed up to share their experiences so we could learn as much as possible from the parent perspective. One topic we asked parents about had to do with what communication they had received. Many responses from parents were similar and show the very problem, structurally, we are facing today in schools.

WHAT COMMUNICATION HAVE YOU RECEIVED ABOUT THE SHIFTS OR CHANGES THAT ARE HAPPENING IN MATH EDUCATION, OR THE WAY WE TEACH MATH, TODAY?

Sample parent responses:

- "Truthfully, I don't think they've done anything."
- "I will be completely honest with you. Not a ton."
- "I actually don't think that much notification has come home about math education at all."
- "I don't think a lot. We've had two parent–teacher conferences with her current teacher, but it's not something that we've talked about."
- "I would say nothing."
- "In terms of an overall picture, not very much, but [we are] kind of informed as changes come . . . and it's very "Oh, this is happening . . . and it's happening tomorrow." Seems like there is not a whole lot of planning."
- "Nightly emails about math homework, but it doesn't tell me about how they learned the math, so by the time I see it I am trying to figure out how to help my child."

We cannot expect parents to magically understand the shifts in mathematics education if our school structures are not providing the education for them. This is why parents resort to searching and learning from "Dr. Google," as one parent called it when asked what she does when something comes home that is unfamiliar to her. Parents also rely on other social media and search engines to gain understanding, because the system that should include them has left them out. Another parent shares their frustration about searching the web for answers:

> *I don't want to undo what he's learned in school, so I have to try figure out what he's doing and the frustration of trying to find that method . . . and even when you look it up [online], it's really difficult to pinpoint it because what his teacher might do with dots and arrays somebody else is doing with boxes. So that is the biggest challenge . . . is trying to match my help with what he's learning in school and there not being any communication to bridge that gap.*

If parents are not using the Internet for help, then they simply are left to rely on their own knowledge, like this parent:

> *I'm not sure how the math was taught and I don't want to introduce a new way of learning it. I'd rather kind of reinforce the way the teacher is doing it, as opposed to teaching it my way. I don't want to confuse my kid, but I end up having to do it my way or how YouTube does it because I don't know how it's being taught.*

Most educators would agree that at the end of the day, all the work we do is for the kids. If this premise is true, then involving and educating parents should be at the forefront of our work, not an afterthought. This is why it is important to ensure that schoolwide structures are in place.

As we have seen, parents play a tremendous role in educating our students. For one, they are a child's first and primary teacher. For this reason, we need them to work *with us*, not against us. Remember, the definition of a system functions on the idea that stakeholders *work together* to operate. This means it falls on us, the educators and the system, to embrace parents, involve them, and educate them. To do this, we have to first identify the structures that need work. One teacher adjusting their classroom structure will certainly improve experiences for *their* classroom parents but will not meet *all* parents' needs for a school. To reach *all* parents, a schoolwide initiative (all teachers and educators, together with administration, and ultimately with parents) needs to occur.

We cannot expect parents to magically understand the shifts in mathematics education if our school structures are not providing the education for them.

Involving and educating parents should be at the forefront of our work, not an afterthought.

Consistent policies and expectations can positively impact communication to and with parents around mathematics.

Schoolwide initiatives focused on parents require school leaders, teachers, and other educators to know and understand their role as it pertains to parents, craft and communicate consistent schoolwide policies, and reflect on their current practices and acknowledge areas where they can improve. They also require us to *all* be committed to doing our part to ensure parents are included and informed. Each person involved in a child's learning needs to understand and commit to doing their share for schoolwide success. Consistent policies and expectations can positively impact communication to and with parents around mathematics.

Though this chapter is focused on schoolwide structures, that does not mean it is not meant for teachers. Teachers are leaders too. While teachers might not be able to directly enact schoolwide policy, they do heavily influence how and what schoolwide structures exist. For this reason, throughout the chapter, we have specifically included tip boxes for teachers to highlight ways to influence larger-scale change beyond the walls of their own classroom or grade-level team.

DETERMINING THE ROLES OF ALL STAKEHOLDERS

It is easy to begin the school year assuming that everyone knows and understands their roles as they relate to addressing parents' mathematics needs. But just like we cannot assume that students in fifth grade know how to work collaboratively in groups (even though they have been doing it for 6 years!), we also cannot assume that all stakeholders understand their role and associated responsibilities in partnering with parents in mathematics. Additionally, sometimes there are new hires, grade-level changes, new or adjusted district/school policies, and new families and students to the school or district, all of which warrant a refresher on understanding roles and responsibilities.

Knowing and understanding your role and the roles of other stakeholders can prevent gaps in communication, redundancy, and conflicting messages. So, who is responsible for each of the parents' four core wants? Which stakeholder(s) ensures parents feel helpful, intelligent, confident, and familiar with the language?

Clarifying the Roles of Leaders, Teachers, and Other Educators

Take a moment to reflect about who in your building or district is responsible for particular tasks. Fill in the person(s) or group you think is responsible for each of the actions listed in the left column. Add other responsibilities that apply to your school context.

Reflect

Roles and Responsibilities	
Who Is Responsible for . . .	**Person(s) or Group Responsible**
1. Choosing communication tools for use with parents?	
2. Informing parents about shifts and changes they can expect in their child's math learning experience as compared to their own or previous children's experiences?	
3. Ensuring mathematics communication is accessible to all parents?	
4. Planning, developing, and implementing in-school and out-of-school math-specific events for parents?	
5. Planning and developing any math-specific information during in-school or out-of-school events nonspecific to math for parents?	
6. Creating letters for parents informing what to expect for the next math unit?	
Add your own.	

online resources ⟋ Available for download at **resources.corwin.com/partneringwithparents/elementary**

Reflect icon source: Vladislav Popov/iStock.com.

TIP!

Are you a teacher or other educator who wants to see schoolwide change? Ask several colleagues to fill out the previous Reflection exercise anonymously. If the answers vary, take the data to your school leader and use the data to guide your discussion about the inconsistency in understandings of roles and responsibilities. Show them that there is a lack of consensus around the roles and responsibilities of educators and school leaders and offer to collaborate on developing solutions, such as co-leading a small task force, committee, or faculty meeting around identifying clear definitions of roles and responsibilities.

Were there any responsibilities that challenged you? Do you think your answers would match your colleagues' answers? If you had colleagues try this Reflect exercise, did their answers match yours? This chart is a quick way to identify whether or not particular roles and responsibilities are clear to school leaders, teachers, and other educators. If the roles are not clear, then you will be able to see some areas where gaps in communication, redundancy, or conflicting messages might be occurring schoolwide.

Knowing your role and responsibilities specific to involving, communicating, and educating parents is critical for schoolwide mathematical success.

Clarifying the Roles of Parents

Equally important to administrators and educators' understanding of their role in a child's mathematics education is parents' understanding of their role. As we shared in the Introduction, we have found that many parents view their role in different ways. Many parents view themselves as their child's coach or mentor. They leave the teaching to the teacher but provide support in various ways to ensure their child is making adequate progress. Some parents take on the role of teacher at home by showing their child how they learned and/or try to follow the class notes to reteach a lesson. Other parents see themselves as disciplinarians who enforce strict homework policies and focus on memorization of basic facts. Many parents adopt a "laissez-faire" approach and believe the math learning only needs to happen in the classroom. While it is great that some parents want to continue the learning at home, and it is equally great that other parents want to let the teachers be the teachers, the inconsistencies in parents' understanding of their role causes many issues.

Because of the lack of shared understanding, some parents might undo their child's learning by teaching them outdated mathematics strategies or processes or show procedures that do not align with the point of learning in the child's current mathematics trajectory. Meanwhile, others might strip away the premise that mathematics is joyful and fun. Schools and districts need to own the responsibility for defining the role and responsibilities of parents, both in their own mathematics learning and in their role as the child's first teacher.

> Schools and districts need to own the responsibility for defining the role and responsibilities of parents, both in their own mathematics learning and in their role as the child's first teacher.

Take a moment to reflect on your personal beliefs of the parents' roles and responsibilities.

Reflect

- What do you believe is a parent's role in their child's mathematics education at your school?

- What would you like parents to do to support their child's mathematics learning?

Now that you have had a moment to reflect about how you define the parents' role, think about the following:

- How do you ensure parents are equipped to feel helpful, confident, intelligent, and familiar with the language (parents' four core wants) at home?
- Have the parents in your school been provided a list of their responsibilities as they pertain to their child's mathematics learning?
- In looking at your list, do you think your list matches parents' understanding?
- Is the role the same whether the student is a kindergartner or a fifth grader? If not, how does it vary?
- How can you communicate the parent's role in their child's learning?

CRAFTING AND COMMUNICATING CONSISTENT SCHOOLWIDE POLICIES

Along with clarification of roles of stakeholders, there also needs to be consistency in both policy about certain topics at the school level and in messaging to parents from the school that conveys those policies and upholds the commitments. One reason this matters is so that students in different grade levels (and their parents) are experiencing similar outcomes and don't have to modify expectations from teacher to teacher, year to year. Also, many parents have multiple children within the same school. Vast differences in the messaging or specific policies between classrooms can be burdensome for parents and ultimately impact the teacher–parent relationship. Our conversations

Reflect icon source: Vladislav Popov/iStock.com.

with parents revealed that in addition to the need for clarification around their responsibilities, two schoolwide structures are a point of contention if they do not have schoolwide, or even grade-level, consistency: expectations and policies around homework and grading. Therefore, we will focus on those two structures, from the mathematics perspective, for the rest of the chapter.

Establishing Homework Policies

At the elementary level, homework is a very controversial topic. To give or not to give homework? That is the question. For teachers, there are a variety of approaches to homework, ranging from assigning a lot of it to assigning none at all, assigning tasks for procedural practice to those meant to bolster conceptual understanding, assigning basic review, and more. One benefit of homework is that it can play a powerful role in engaging parents more deeply in the content their child is learning; it can provide a starting point for a mathematical conversation (Walker, Hoover-Dempsey, Whetsel, & Green, 2004).

However, homework can have many challenges as well. Foremost is that homework can be a question of equity. Students have varying assets such as time availability, prior knowledge, access to technology and other resources, and more. The same is true for their parents. Some families are able to establish consistent homework routines and working environments for their children; in some households, children are left to their own devices.

Another challenge for parents is frustration caused by inconsistent policies around the quality and amount of homework, specifically in mathematics. Parking lot conversations often begin with venting about the amount of homework assigned and comparing it to what other children have. For parents with more than one child in a school, inconsistent messaging between teachers creates strife at home. And if policies and expectations shift from year to year, children and parents often end up confused and have to constantly shift routines and habits, which leads to upheaval and stress. This is especially challenging for younger children.

Despite the best intentions, homework can have negative impacts if there is not a shared vision around the purpose, amount, and role. According to the National Parent Teacher Association (2016),

Homework has the potential to negatively impact family and child interactions, and high quantities of homework not only add to stress, but do not necessarily lead to higher achievement outcomes; additionally research has proven that students who spend more than the recommended grade appropriate time on homework can experience no increase or a decrease in academic achievement.

We are not advocating that your school should choose to assign or not assign homework. But we do argue that to best support children's learning and engagement, and to prevent parental frustration, there should be schoolwide consistency and agreement on the following:

- The purpose of homework
- The amount and frequency of homework assigned per grade level
- The role of the student, teacher/school, and parent in homework

In addition to agreement, these policies need to include parent voices in policy development or adjustment and they should be clearly communicated.

Tips If Your School Lacks a Consistent Homework Policy

Are you a teacher in a school that lacks a schoolwide homework policy? One suggestion is to collaborate with your grade-level team to create one consistent grade-level message about homework, including its purpose, amount, and frequency. This way, if parents have multiple children in the same grade, they only have one policy by which to adhere. Sometimes schoolwide change has to start at the classroom level and work its way up. Once you have tried to create grade-level consensus, you can approach your school leader and suggest something similar be done schoolwide or you can set up a meeting with an adjacent grade level to see if they will enact a similar policy. If for some reason you cannot get grade-level consensus, consider asking your school leader to define for you their expectations around homework and consider using their recommendation as what you communicate to parents and by which you abide.

Purpose of Homework

Homework at the elementary level can serve a variety of purposes. Take a moment and think about why mathematics homework is assigned in your building or classroom.

> ## Is the Purpose of the Homework to . . .
>
> - Help students develop study skills and habits?
> - Keep families informed about their child's learning?
> - Provide additional practice for basic skills?
> - Review previously taught concepts?
> - Prepare students for upcoming topics?
> - Extend student thinking?

Homework can have negative impacts if there is not a shared vision around the purpose, amount, and role.

Perhaps you identified one or more of these reasons for assigning homework. The question then becomes, is there consensus in your building around the responses? Do all the teachers in the same building agree on the rationale for assigning (or not assigning) mathematics homework, and do they stick to that agreement? If so, great! If not, how can you use your power of influence to begin to identify ways to develop schoolwide consistency around *why* homework is or is not assigned?

Amount of Homework

Each school or district determines their own policy around how much homework a teacher should assign and how long students should be spending on homework daily. The National Parent Teacher Association and the National Education Association set recommendations that align with revered homework researcher Dr. Harris Cooper's findings (Cooper, 1989). In their recommendations, they suggest adhering to 10 minutes per grade level daily (e.g., 20 minutes for second grade, 50 minutes for fifth grade) (National Education Association, 2015). This recommendation includes all core subject areas.

Overall, it really comes back to the question of purpose. Why is your school assigning mathematics homework? If it is for basic skill review, then 5–10 minutes daily per grade level is a reasonable expectation. If it is about helping parents see what their child is learning, then the amount of homework might be an example of the model or strategy used in class, along with one or two tasks that ask the child to show understanding. If it is about extending student thinking, then perhaps the assignment becomes a long-term project that asks students to do a task over the course of a week. This gives students choice in determining how much time they want to spend and how frequently they want to work on the assignment. It also teaches them time management. For all these reasons, we encourage teachers and other educators to match their homework practices with their purpose for giving the homework.

Communicating Expectations for Parent Involvement

As discussed previously, for parents to be most successful as a partner, they need to understand the role they play in all aspects of their child's mathematics learning—including homework if your school or district assigns it. If the district or school puts out guidelines stating how long homework should take, what is the expectation for what the parent should do if the child takes longer (e.g., the recommendation is 40 minutes but the child regularly spends 60 minutes)? Or what if a child does not remember how they solved a particular problem that they have been assigned? How should a parent proceed to support their youngster? What is the student's role? Does everyone know their role?

In the situation where the suggested maximum time spent on a high-quality assignment is exceeded, we suggest parents should be encouraged to sign off on the homework or send a note to the teacher confirming that the child attempted the work in good faith. Depending on the grade level, we also suggest having the student write a note to the teacher. This will provide the teacher with formative feedback on what parts were most approachable (and often easiest) for the student versus what they did not get to or avoided. If the parent steps in and shows their child what to do, the teacher will likely receive inaccurate information. Establishing this guideline early on can help to build positive relationships between the teacher, student, and parent and reinforce particular school norms, such as fostering a growth mindset. In addition, it will limit the temptation for parents to show their child how to solve it "their way," which often leads to more confusion and frustration, especially in the upper grades.

For all of this to work, a clear and concise policy, along with communication of those roles and responsibilities, needs to be provided from the start of school. Take a look at Figure 3.1 to see an example of a simple chart that can be provided to all stakeholders at the beginning of the year so they understand each and every role, including their own. This chart can easily be added to a student–parent and faculty handbook. In Chapter 5, we discuss at a more granular level what to communicate with parents when, and we show how this chart can be adapted specifically for communicating with parents about their role.

Figure 3.1 – Roles and Responsibilities With Math Homework

Student, Parent, Teacher, and Administrator Roles With Homework			
Students	**Parents**	**Teachers**	**Administrators**
• Know what the assignments are • Complete assignments on time • Put forth best effort • Let the teacher know if they do not understand an assignment or will have difficulty completing it on time	As best as they can . . . • Know what the assignments are • Provide the child a safe and quiet workspace • Convey a positive attitude in front of their child about math and school • Establish clear homework routines • Provide guidance, not answers • Watch for signs of frustration and provide breaks • Allow their child to hand in an incomplete assignment • Help the child write a note to the teacher letting them know exactly what the child does not understand or asking for more time to complete it	• Assign high-quality assignments that fall within the school's policy, differentiating as needed • Ensure homework is written in agenda notebooks and/or on the class website • State the purpose of the assignment for parents and students • Provide clear directions and exemplars, where applicable • Clarify what students need to do to demonstrate that the assignment has been completed • Review homework in a timely manner and provide feedback • Contact parents if homework is not received	• Communicate clear and concise norms and expectations for all stakeholders at the beginning of year • Monitor the implementation of school policy • Survey families to determine if the amount of time spent on homework is too much, too little, or just right and their perceived quality of assignments • Work with school staff to identify students at risk who may need additional supports or resources to complete homework

Source: Based on Bembenutty, H. (2011). The last word: An interview with Harris Cooper—research, policies, tips, and current perspectives on homework. *Journal of Advanced Academics,* 22(2), 340–349.

 Available for download at **resources.corwin.com/partneringwithparents/elementary**

Overall, ensuring there is a consistent schoolwide policy regarding homework assignments and a clear understanding of the roles will help prevent parent frustration. At a minimum, teachers in a school that has yet to reach schoolwide consensus should be as transparent with parents as possible about what to expect as far as homework assignments. To see example correspondence about homework and the policies, be sure to read Chapter 5 where we dive deeper into communication with parents.

Communicating Grading Policies

Communicating grading policies is equally as important as communicating homework policies. Whether your school uses traditional or standards-based grading, policies and rubrics need to be made transparent for parents so they can understand exactly what is expected of their child.

Traditional Grading

Some schools still make use of traditional grading systems (e.g., "Excellent, Very Good, Good, Satisfactory, Unsatisfactory" or A–F letter grading and 100-point numerical systems). Many parents are accustomed to traditional grading since they grew up with it. Even though parents may be familiar with the grading policy itself, it is still helpful to be forthright about how they can use the grades to inform their understanding of their child's progress. In addition, helping parents understand the policies on retakes, missed assignments, and extra credit can help them better support their child.

Tips for Helping Students and Parents Understand Your Grading Policy

- Be clear at the beginning of the year about what your grading rubric looks like (e.g., 30% of the grade is marked by quizzes/tests, 10% by participation, etc.).
- Because traditional grading does not specify standards, be sure to outline what the learning outcomes were for the period being assessed so parents have a general understanding of what parts of the mathematics their child did well or struggled with.
- Provide both students and parents examples of what would be considered an "A" or excellent, a "B" or very good, and so on.
- Reinforce that a grade does not indicate someone's future success in a subject and that receiving less than an "A" does not mean that a student is bad at math.

Standards-Based Grading

While some school districts still use traditional grading structures for reporting progress to parents, many school districts have switched to standards-based grading, especially at elementary levels. **Standards-based grading** is the idea that students are graded based on their progress over time for particular topics and standards using proficiency levels as measures of achievement, as opposed to the traditional measure of achievement found by averaging grades over a specific period of time to find one distinct grade. Standards-based grading can often be a sticking point for parents due to its novelty.

Standards-Based Grading: Students are graded based on their progress over time for particular topics and standards using proficiency levels as measures of achievement, as opposed to the traditional measure of achievement found by averaging grades over a specific period of time to find one distinct grade.

When districts and schools make a systemic shift of this nature, it is critical that all stakeholders understand the change. Parents, the target receivers of the information contained on the report cards, generally do not understand standards-based grading and often still apply their traditional understanding of averaging numbers to this approach, defeating the purpose of the standards-based grading. To combat misunderstandings, districts and schools generally send home accompanying pamphlets and letters to help support parent understanding, but oftentimes this is not enough. So, how can you communicate these changes in a way in which parents will receive it?

Let us start by comparing the elementary math report cards of yesteryear to today. Figure 3.2 shows what parents might have received in 1997 with regard to the entire status of their third-grade child's mathematics understanding. For comparison, Figure 3.3 shows only a small excerpt of what parents may have received in 2020. Take a moment and think about what you notice and what you wonder about the two report cards.

Reflect

Look at the two different forms of recording grades shown in Figures 3.2 and 3.3 on the next page. Write your noticings and wonderings in the chart provided.

Noticings	Wonderings
•	•
•	•
•	•

Reflect icon source: Vladislav Popov/iStock.com.

Figure 3.2 – Elementary Math Grade 3 Report Card From 1997

Mathematics	
Understands Concepts	E
Knows Basic Number Facts	VG
Reasons Well in Problem-Solving	G
Key: E = Excellent, VG = Very Good, G = Good, S = Satisfactory, NI = Needs Improvement, U = Unsatisfactory	

Figure 3.3 – Excerpt From Elementary Math Grade 3 Report Card From 2020

Mathematics	
Number and Operations in Base Ten	
Understands base-ten place value system for whole numbers.	**Meeting**
Adds and subtracts multidigit whole numbers accurately.	**Meeting**
Multiplies and divides multidigit whole numbers accurately.	**Developing**
Understands rounding of whole numbers based on place value.	**Beginning**

Key:

Exceeding Understanding of Standard

The student independently and consistently demonstrates advanced understanding of end-of-year grade-level standards. To exceed understanding of a standard, a student must show high-quality work reflecting higher-level thinking skills. *In some cases, it will be indicated that it is not possible to work beyond "Meeting Understanding."*

Meeting Understanding of Standard

The student demonstrates proficiency in the topic. To meet understanding of a standard, a student must apply skills and strategies with accuracy and quality independently. Meeting Understanding is the goal for all students to achieve.

Developing Understanding of Standard

The student is making progress in the indicated topic. To develop understanding of a standard, a student must apply skills and strategies with varied consistency, quality, and support.

Beginning Understanding of Standard

The student has a beginning understanding of the specific topic. To have a beginning understanding of a standard, a student performs inconsistently and shows limited application of skills and strategies. Student requires considerable support and guidance.

Not Assessed at This Time

The standard has not yet been assessed.

Now take a moment and compare your noticings and wonderings to ours (Figure 3.4).

Figure 3.4 – Report Card Noticings and Wonderings

Noticings	Wonderings
• Figure 3.3 is much more detailed than Figure 3.2. • Figure 3.2 has six grading categories, while Figure 3.3 has only four. • Figure 3.3 specifies the content area being studied (Numbers and Operations in Base Ten). • Figure 3.3 details what each indicator means, while Figure 3.2 does not. • Figure 3.3 states that the rating of exemplary may not always be possible. • Figure 3.3 shows that sometimes parents will see "N/A" for not assessed at this time. • Figure 3.2 is simpler and shorter.	• What makes "Good" different from "Satisfactory" on the traditional report card? Likewise, what makes "Very Good" different from "Excellent" or "Good"? • How can a parent know how to help their child with the traditional report card given it provides little to no specifics? • What topic or standard is the report card in Figure 3.2 assessing? • What might the report card in Figure 3.3 have for assessing problem-solving? • How can we help parents understand why a student cannot receive Exceeding Understanding for some standards?

There is little debate as to which report card gives more detailed information about a child's progress. Traditional report cards state only a grade, such as "E" for "Excellent" and "VG" for "Very Good" or the more recognizable letter grades (A, A-, B+, etc.). These traditional report cards offer virtually no information for the parent as to their child's strengths and areas of struggle, nor do they specify the content topic or standard. With a standards-based report card, parents are able to see a child's progress toward specific mathematical domains and/or individual standards or topics on a proficiency scale. However, sometimes report cards contain educational jargon or are not easy to understand, resulting in additional parent struggle.

It can be helpful to include this very activity in the school or district pamphlet on report cards. Ask parents to compare and contrast a mathematics report card of the past to today so they can appreciate the specificity and adjustments made to keep them more informed. If you are a teacher and more details are not provided schoolwide for parents, offer your classroom of parents this opportunity by proactively including what to expect regarding report cards in your beginning of the year correspondence or in addition to the school or district resources sent out with report cards. By providing parents this level of information early in the school year, parent–teacher conferences usually held later in the year can be more productive discussions of the details of each child's growth, as these events can often be used to communicate grading policies. Read more about hosting parent events in Chapter 6.

Without educating parents about how to read and interpret the standards-based report cards, parents may end up feeling confused, worried, frustrated, or unintelligent and thus unable to help their child make adequate progress. These are the same feelings they often display about the way we teach math today.

Particularly, parents have shared frustration about the inability for their child to consistently exceed expectations on all standards. This frustration stems from a lack of understanding about standards-based grading and reporting. For parents to fully understand this, it requires looking through a different lens and helping them to adjust their own understanding of the purpose and premise for grading.

We suggest providing parents a real-world comparison to help them understand the standards-based competencies. Here's an example. In many cases, such as taking a driver's test, graduating medical school, or getting an occupational license, there are generally two options: pass or fail. Sure someone can do better than meeting the standard on their driver's test or on their performance on an occupational licensure exam, but what is *assessed* is the level of proficiency needed to be competent at a particular skill. It is then equally as critical that parents are informed that qualitative feedback from teachers will come throughout the year in a variety of forms and that the comments section of the report card provides additional information to families.

> ## Tips for Reporting About Mathematics Progress With Parents
>
> - Include on the district website, associated pamphlet, or other correspondence *why* we use this reporting system as compared to more traditional-style report cards (including a comparative picture, such as Figures 3.2 and 3.3, or a relatable analogy such as our driver's test example, may prove helpful);
> - Write in parent-friendly language and include little to no educational jargon;
> - Provide as much detail and specificity as possible, whether using standards-based or traditional grading systems, so parents have a sense of where their child is along the math learning continuum;
> - Explain that "Meeting a Standard" does not equate to "average" but rather where students should be; many parents fear that if the child is not exceeding at a standard, then they are "average" and therefore behind;
> - If your district uses numbers for standards-based grading, specify that it is not comparative to traditional letter grading (e.g., a 4 ≠ A, 3 ≠ B, etc.) but instead is competency based; and
> - Emphasize the importance of the teacher's assessment of student work habits (e.g., organization, time management, effort, perseverance, classroom conduct).

Keep in mind that communication around progress goes well beyond the report card. In Chapter 4, you will explore *how* to enhance your communication. In Chapter 5, you will examine communication at all levels (schoolwide, classwide, individual), and we offer suggestions for how to communicate student progress in mathematics apart from report cards.

GETTING BUY-IN AND COMMITMENT FROM ALL STAKEHOLDERS

Once you have reflected on the roles and responsibilities of school leaders, educators, and parents and analyzed communication policies, it is important to also reflect on shared agreements that might exist. Commitments ensure there is consistency across school leaders, teachers, and other educators, which then allows for regularity in communication across parents. Given that many parents have multiple children, it is essential that there is some constancy in their mathematics experience.

What commitments have you and your colleagues agreed on with regard to addressing parents' mathematics needs? How do you and your colleagues address parents' four core wants? The next Reflect box offers two examples to get you started. Take some time to reflect and fill in the table with shared agreements that you as a school have established.

Reflect

Schoolwide Commitments to Addressing Parents' Mathematics Needs
• e.g., Model a mathematical growth mindset in front of students and parents.
• e.g., Host one math-specific event each year.
•

online resources ▸ Available for download at **resources.corwin.com/partneringwithparents/elementary**

Whether you are a school leader or a teacher, if you struggled to identify shared schoolwide commitments or any commitments at all, then this serves as useful data. These data provide a great starting point to communicate as a group and consider what steps need to be taken to ensure there is a collective vision about mathematics teaching and learning with parents in mind and to identify how you can collaborate as a group to create change.

Take a moment to reflect on what *you* would like to commit to doing to address parents' mathematics needs. Be sure to be specific: what are the commitments and how do those commitments happen? Here are two examples to get you started.

Reflect icon source: Vladislav Popov/iStock.com.

Reflect

Personal Commitments to Addressing Parents' Mathematics Needs

- *e.g., Survey parents to understand where they are in their understanding of today's math and to learn about their mindset.*
- *e.g., Provide parents a brief document in the beginning of every school year outlining what they can expect their child to learn mathematically and what skills they should have by the end of the year.*

-

 Available for download at **resources.corwin.com/partneringwithparents/elementary**

Your personal commitments can be the start of the schoolwide commitments your school makes. Ask your colleagues to do this same exercise and you will find you have lots of commitments from which to choose! Remember, schoolwide commitments are those that *all* stakeholders agree to and uphold. Therefore, if you use your personal commitments as a starting place, be sure there are plenty of opportunities for your colleagues to have their voice heard.

For ease, we have provided you with a sample schoolwide commitment focused specifically on addressing parents' mathematics needs (Figure 3.5).

Reflect icon source: Vladislav Popov/iStock.com.

Figure 3.5 – Sample Schoolwide Commitments

Sample Schoolwide Commitments for Addressing Parents' Mathematics Needs

Administration

I Commit to . . .

- Communicating the school's expectations to teachers and staff, defining their role and responsibilities as they pertain to informing and communicating with parents mathematically.
- Sending schoolwide communication to parents and guardians stating the school's expectations as it pertains to their roles, responsibilities, and mathematical learning journey.
- Providing teachers and staff the appropriate resources (time or materials) for engaging parents in their mathematical learning.
- Ensuring all communication to parents is accessible (translated, printed, and digital).
- Hosting one event centered around why math instruction has changed for parents and to make all information accessible in a timely manner for those who cannot attend.
- Developing a shared vision around what we value for high-quality mathematics teaching and learning, with voices from all stakeholders.
- Guaranteeing policies and procedures are clear and consistent schoolwide.

Teachers and Instructional/Math Coaches

I Commit to . . .

- Promoting a growth mindset and redirecting negative or fixed mindset talk.
- Sending home a letter at the beginning of the year (co-written with my grade-level team) that addresses that the way we teach mathematics may be different than what parents experienced and state why, indicates topics that will be covered throughout the year, and advises that more specific letters will be sent home before every new topic.
- Sending home a beginning of year attitudinal survey (similar to the Chapter 1 Apply It! exercise) to assess parents' feelings toward and experiences in math and their at-home supports in math.
- Sending home specific one- to two-page letters before each new topic, outlining (a) what the child will learn in layman's terms; (b) new terminology that parents might hear or see, along with associated definitions; (c) new tools or representations that parents might see; and (d) an explanation for why their children are learning that topic in math in a different way than parents might have experienced it. (This will be covered in Chapter 5.)
- Communicating student progress to parents often and in a variety of ways. (This will be covered in Chapter 5.)

(Continued)

(*Continued*)

Sample Schoolwide Commitments for Addressing Parents' Mathematics Needs

Parents and Guardians

I Commit to . . .

- Reading information sent home from my child's teacher.
- Asking my child's teacher for help or more information when I am unsure about a topic or want to understand my child's progress.
- Allowing my child to submit incomplete homework if they struggle, so long as they have put in their best effort, with a written note to their teacher explaining their struggles.
- Reinforcing the teacher's methods, not teaching my child math the way I learned it (unless that is how they are learning it).
- Speaking positively about math around and in front of my child.
- Helping my child notice math around them and in the real world.

online resources — Available for download at **resources.corwin.com/partneringwithparents/elementary**

Use this sample commitment form if it aligns with the work your stakeholders commit to, or work with your colleagues to develop your own. Either way, this form is meant to hold all stakeholders accountable for their part of the system. If you are a school leader, consider putting together a group of educators and parents to co-create commitments such as the ones in Figure 3.5. If you are a teacher or other educator, consider bringing this sample commitment form to your school leaders and asking how your school can move toward creating consistency between and among stakeholders about parents' mathematics needs. This type of document can be included in the student–parent handbook (along with the faculty handbook) or in beginning of the year correspondence.

Creating a list of stakeholder commitments ensures that schoolwide expectations are in place for consistency, specifically around parent communication about mathematics. It is not uncommon for us to hear from parents that "So-and-so was a great teacher because of x, y, and z," rather than "Our school is great because of x, y, and z." We believe this often occurs as a direct result of lacking shared commitments and a common understanding of who is responsible for ensuring parents feel helpful, intelligent, confident, and familiar with the language (parents' four core wants).

For more resources on creating shared mathematics visions and cohesive schoolwide mathematics agreements about mathematics teaching and learning, we suggest reading the following resources:

- *The Math Pact: Achieving Instructional Coherence Within and Across Grades, Elementary* by Karen S. Karp, Barbara J. Dougherty, and Sarah B. Bush (2020)
- *Essential Actions Series: Framework for Leadership in Mathematics Education* by NCSM Leadership in Mathematics Education (2020)

PUTTING IT ALL TOGETHER

In this chapter, you thought deeply about how clarifying the roles and responsibilities of school leaders, teachers, and parents is key to consistency. You also pondered ways in which to ensure structures are in place in your own school or district so that parents are provided more information with regard to policies and expectations around homework and report cards. In the next chapter, you will explore *how* to communicate with parents about mathematics in more detail.

FREQUENTLY ASKED QUESTIONS

Q My school has a schoolwide policy to assign homework daily, but I don't believe it is effective to give students in elementary school math homework. What should I do?

A We understand that sometimes schoolwide policies do not equate to schoolwide agreement. First, we suggest researching your claim. What evidence do you have to support that assigning elementary students homework is not effective? Then, it is important for you to use your power of influence as a teacher to bring the research to school leaders and have crucial conversations centered on the purpose of homework in your building. While you push for schoolwide consensus, perhaps you can think about how you can assign homework that builds students' independence or focuses more on their mathematical habits rather than the content itself (for example, mathematical perseverance or precision).

Q My school uses standards-based grading and honestly I
don't really understand it myself. Sometimes teachers
find it just as confusing as parents do. What can I do?

A Professional learning opportunities are important for educators
when change occurs. We suggest checking in with school leaders
to see if a session was held upon the switch from traditional grading
to standards-based grading that you might have missed. Alternatively,
we suggest reading about the history of grading and the ideas behind
standards-based grading. Some resources to look into are as follows:

- *The Standards-Based Classroom: Making Learning the Goal* by
  Emily Rinkema and Stan Williams (2018)
- *Developing Standards-Based Report Cards* by Thomas R.
  Guskey and Jane M. Bailey (2009)
- *Charting a Course to Standards-Based Grading: What to Stop,
  What to Start, and Why It Matters* by Tim R. Westerberg (2016)
- *A School Leader's Guide to Standards-Based Grading* by Tammy
  Heflebower, Jan K. Hoegh, and Phil Warrick, with Mitzi
  Hoback, Margaret McInteer, and Bev Clemens (2014)

APPLY IT! TEACHER ACTIVITIES

How Will Your School Commit to the Work of Addressing Parent Needs With Regard to Mathematics Teaching and Learning?

1. Look back at Figure 3.5. What is one commitment listed there
   that is new for you? Brainstorm how you could work to make
   that a commitment for yourself.
2. Think about what from this chapter you wish your administration
   would consider in regard to approaches for mathematical
   instruction. How could you develop an action plan to help
   facilitate this necessary change within your team or school?

 Available for download at **resources.corwin.com/partneringwithparents/
elementary**

Apply It! icon source: PeterSnow/iStock.com.

APPLY IT! SCHOOL LEADER ACTIVITIES

How Will Your School Commit to the Work of Addressing Parent Needs With Regard to Mathematics Teaching and Learning?

1. Survey your staff to find out what consensus you currently have around homework. Some suggested questions are listed below.

[Name of School] Homework Policy Survey

What is [Name of School]'s purpose for assigning mathematics homework?

☐ Computational practice

☐ Preparation for upcoming lessons

☐ Extension opportunities

☐ Developing study habits

☐ Basic skills review

How frequently should [Name of School] Grade ___ teachers assign homework?

☐ Daily

☐ Two or three times a week

☐ Once a week

☐ Long-term assignments only

What amount of homework should [Name of School] Grade ___ teachers assign?

☐ 5–10 minutes

☐ 11–20 minutes

☐ 21–30 minutes

(Continued)

Apply It! icon source: PeterSnow/iStock.com.

(Continued)

☐ 31–40 minutes

☐ 41–50 minutes

☐ 51–60 minutes

☐ 1 hour or more

online resources ☐ Available for download at **resources.corwin.com/partneringwithparents/ elementary**

2. Give Figure 3.5 (Schoolwide Commitments for Addressing Parents' Mathematics Needs) to your staff at a faculty meeting. Have the faculty then meet in heterogeneous groups to identify similarities and differences among their responses. Then, as a whole group, brainstorm ways for the school to reach consensus. Leave with an action plan for creating schoolwide norms around roles and responsibilities with regard to mathematics teaching and learning—with parents in mind.

CHAPTER 4

Exploring *How* to Communicate With Parents About Math

Communication is your ticket to success, if you pay attention and learn to do it effectively.

— Theo Gold

As we saw in Chapter 2, understanding *what* parents want to know is a critical part of effectively communicating with them. It is important to remember that the goal is not to develop parents into teachers, but rather to provide them enough information to meet their four core wants. Parents want to be able to feel helpful, intelligent, confident, and familiar with the language so they can communicate with their child in a way that does not feel like they are speaking two different languages. Once it is understood *what* parents want to know to be productive partners and there is schoolwide clarity and commitment on policy and messaging, then *how* to communicate with parents about mathematics teaching and learning becomes more effective.

Communication is all about relationships. In this chapter, as you consider how you communicate with families, think about how you have built or plan to

> ## IN THIS CHAPTER YOU WILL . . .
>
> - Explore what makes written communication with parents effective,
> - Consider various methods and tools used to communicate with parents, and
> - Reflect on *how* you can enhance your communication about mathematics with parents.

Icon source: Momento Design/iStock.com.

> Once it is understood *what* parents want to know to be productive partners and there is schoolwide clarity and commitment on policy and messaging, then *how* to communicate with parents about mathematics teaching and learning becomes more effective.

build relationships with them. It is important to keep in mind that communication is not one size fits all and what works for one parent may not work for others. Similarly, what might work for one school and region may not work for a different school in a different region. Use this chapter to help you reflect on how you and your school as a whole communicate with families about mathematics.

WHAT MAKES WRITTEN COMMUNICATION WITH PARENTS *EFFECTIVE*?

As George Bernard Shaw once said, "The single biggest problem in communication is the illusion that it has taken place." If the education community at large has been *effectively* communicating with families about math, then we hypothesize that we wouldn't see memes and social media posts like those in Figure 4.1. Nor would we hear from parents we interview that they do not understand why math instruction has changed, among other complaints about not receiving enough information.

Figure 4.1 – Memes and Social Media Posts About Math

Source: Created with imgflip.com.

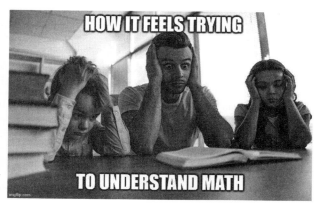

Source: M-image/iStock.com. Created with imgflip.com.

In our experience working with educators, we have yet to hear any educator who feels they communicate too little with families. Yet we frequently hear from families that they feel they are underinformed. So, where is the divide?

As you walk through this chapter, reflect on your own communication with families.

Reflect

QUESTIONS YOU MAY WANT TO THINK ABOUT

- How do you know parents have received your communication?

- How do you know they have read it?

- How do you know they have understood it?

- How do you ensure your communication is accessible for all parents?

- How often do you communicate?

We believe that effective written communication is

- Written so parents can read it,
- Written so parents want to read it,
- Written so it relates to what parents know, and
- Done frequently and proactively.

There are many ways to make ongoing written communication more effective with parents. The first is to ensure that your communication is accessible. Not all parents speak English as a first language and not all parents are literate, so our communication must be crafted carefully to ensure the recipient can access it.

Write So They Can Read It

Did you know that approximately 36 million adults in America read, write, or do basic math at or below a third-grade level (ProLiteracy, 2018)? According to the most recent national assessment of adult literacy, 52% of the U.S. adult population has basic or below average reading proficiency (U.S. Department of Education, 2017). For these reasons, it is ever more important that our communication with parents is written in a way that can be received. Given these data, it is recommended that written materials be presented at no higher than an eighth-grade reading level, with most recommendations suggesting a sixth-grade reading level for a general audience. Of course, knowing your population of parents will help you make the best determination for the appropriate reading level of your written correspondence.

When we (the authors) write correspondence to families, we largely aim to use readability formulas that provide us a general baseline for whether our written language is simple enough to be read by the majority of adults. Readability scores are generated by formulas that measure the difficulty (or lack thereof) of written materials, such as vocabulary and sentence construction. Though the formulas vary depending on which one you use, they primarily work by estimating the difficulty of countable things, such as length of words and sentences. We use the Grammarly application as our main tool to determine readability scores, and we sometimes use Microsoft Word's Flesch–Kincaid formulas as well.

> **TIP!**
>
> We love to use the Grammarly Chrome Extension application for providing a quick readability score. The application is user-friendly and free for accessing readability scores, and it can easily be added as an extension to your Chrome browser for use in word-processing documents such as Google Docs or Microsoft Word.

We recommend adhering to the guidelines and cautions put forth by the U.S. Department of Health and Human Services (2010) for readability formulas, such as the ones behind applications like Grammarly or word-processing packages like Microsoft Word. Though readability formulas are helpful, they are computer generated and not always accurate. In addition, the results can vary from test to test and they can ignore factors that contribute to ease of reading. That being said, if readability formulas are used and interpreted appropriately, they can be useful in our communication to families as a general baseline for us to use as guidance toward further refining our writing.

Take a look at Figure 4.2, where we show how we used two different readability applications to help us adjust our wording on a family letter we will describe in more detail in Chapter 5.

Figure 4.2 – Example Correspondence to Families

Before	After
Dear Families,	Dear Families,
Welcome to Grade __ mathematics! We are excited to be working with you and your child this year to help enhance your child's love of mathematics learning. Mathematics is critical to one's future success, so we hope to help your child see themselves as mathematicians who find value in learning the subject. To do this, we will build a strong foundation in problem-solving, conceptual understanding, and procedural fluency and topics will be taught so that they build on previous understanding and prepare students for their future math learning.	Welcome to Grade __ math! We are excited to work with you and your child to build your child's love of math learning. Our number one goal is to help your child see themselves as mathematical thinkers who see value in learning math. We also want to help your child see that math is everywhere! To do this, our year-long topics will be taught so that they build on previous understanding and prepare students for future math learning. We will also show students how math is used in the real world.
Readability: This text is likely to be understood by a reader who has at least a ninth-grade education (age 15). (Grammarly Readability app)	**Readability:** This text is simple and easy to read. It's likely to be understood by someone with at least a sixth-grade education (age 11). (Grammarly Readability app)
Flesch–Kincaid Grade Level: 11.6 (Microsoft Word)	**Flesch–Kincaid Grade Level:** 5.9 (Microsoft Word)

As you can see from Figure 4.2, the two readability applications did not necessarily agree with each other, but both helped us to think more about our word choice. We did not take the scores given as quintessential, but rather used them to guide our thinking and help us to see a potential need for revision. The tools helped us to rethink our sentence development and word choice, as we found simpler words that a general reader is more likely to know and we simplified some of our more complicated sentences.

Whether you are an administrator or educator, your role includes providing written communication to families. Take a moment and try the activity in Figure 4.3 yourself. Use a letter or passage you wrote previously for parental distribution, or one you are currently working on, and try to simplify the language so it is "readable" to a more general audience.

Figure 4.3 – Try It! Making Your Correspondence Easier to Read

Before	After

Readability: Readability:

Grammarly Readability: Grammarly Readability:

Flesch–Kincaid Grade Level: Flesch–Kincaid Grade Level:

Part of readability is also remembering that many parents are not educators and therefore do not speak what is often referred to as **eduspeak**, or educator jargon. In fact, even individuals who play a dual role as an educator and parent may not teach mathematics and/or elementary school and therefore may still find mathematical eduspeak confusing. Knowing this, math educators need to be deliberate about how we share our messages to ensure that educational jargon is used as infrequently as possible or is accompanied by an explanation and visual. For example, if we are informing parents about mathematics strategies or topics, we might need to use terms that are unfamiliar. While the need to use some precise terminology can drive up readability scores, you can make your communication clear by explaining the terms you are using.

Eduspeak: Jargon often used by educators that is not widely known outside of education.

For example, if you are writing to parents about the addition strategy of using partial sums, be sure you define the mathematical terms and use visuals to support them. In your definition, try not to introduce other new mathematical language that you will *also* have to define. In other words, avoid defining partial sums as the sum of part of a sequence or series of terms. You will then have to define the words *sequence*, *series*, and *terms*!

Look at Figure 4.4 to see how you could take something written for educators and make it accessible for parents.

Once you have written your document in a way you are sure can be read, make sure you provide the content in the languages most accessible for parents. Parents deserve the opportunity to read information in their native language, especially if the end goal is for them to understand the information. Many schools and districts offer translation services, so check with your school or district to see what services are available. The next best solution for a quick (albeit not always fully accurate) turnaround is to input your English text into an online translation service such as Google Translate. It is important to note that math equations and symbols may be hard for the computer to translate or they may not translate correctly at all. Be cautious about computer translations—but if they are your only option, they are better than nothing.

Overall, using simpler language with which a more general audience may be familiar helps the reader understand what is being read.

Figure 4.4 – From Eduspeak to Parentspeak

Eduspeak	Parentspeak
This week your child will use partial sums to add two-digit whole numbers.	This week your child will learn to add two numbers between 10 and 99 using a strategy called **partial sums**. Reminder: a **sum** in math is the total, or result, of adding numbers.
Partial sums is a strategy you can use to add multidigit numbers by adding one place value at a time and then combining the totals.	When using **partial sums**, break apart each number into smaller parts and then combine all the parts to find the total. This week, we will break apart the numbers by place value (tens and ones). In the future, your child might break apart the numbers differently.

Partial sums steps:

1. Rewrite each addend in expanded form.

2. Add, working one place value at a time.

3. Find the sum of each place value.

Example:

$$45 + 56$$

$$45 = 40 + 5$$
$$+ 56 = 50 + 6$$
$$\overline{101 = 90 + 11}$$

How your child might talk about it:

$$45 + 56$$

I can break apart each number by place value:

$45 = 40 + 5$ and $56 = 50 + 6$.

I can add the tens: $40 + 50 = 90$

I can add the ones: $5 + 6 = 11$

I can add the parts: $90 + 11 = 101$

What it might look like mathematically:

$$45 + 56$$

$$45 = 40 + 5$$
$$+ 56 = 50 + 6$$
$$\overline{101 = 90 + 11}$$

At the end of the week, talk with your child about using **partial sums** to add by asking them to show you how to find the total for $39 + 57$ using this strategy. If they struggle, ask these questions:

- Do you think the answer will be greater or less than 100? Why?

- How can you rewrite 39 as tens and ones?

- How can you rewrite 57 as tens and ones?

- What do you get when you add the tens and the tens? The ones and the ones?

- Can you draw your base-ten blocks to help you?

Write So They *Want* to Read It

It is important that *all* communication, whether schoolwide, classwide, or individual, is written so parents want to read it. Remember, the four core wants capture what parents (in general) are looking for when it comes to information: they want to feel **helpful**, **intelligent**, **confident**, and **familiar with the language**. Ask yourself the following questions each and every time you send something home about mathematics:

- Will parents find this *helpful*?

- Will this help parents feel more *intelligent* or *knowledgeable?*

- Will this make parents more *confident*?

- Will this help parents feel more *familiar* with the language and vocabulary?

When you are writing so parents want to read what is written, it is important to remember that parents come from all walks of life. Many parents have an aversion to school, or math in particular, due to their own lived experiences. Because of this, it is even more important that communication be written from a strengths-based perspective. **Strengths-based communication** showcases students' strengths and strong points, a collection of assets, that act as points on which to build. Strengths-based communication is the opposite of deficit-based communication, or the focus on student weaknesses and what a student lacks. Strengths-based communication "recognizes the learner as valuable, competent, and important" (Kobett & Karp, 2020, p. 2).

> **Strengths-based communication** showcases students' strengths and strong points, a collection of assets, that act as points on which to build.

As Kobett and Karp (2020) ask in their book *Strengths-Based Teaching and Learning in Mathematics*, "What if we regularly were only told what we don't do well?" Now apply that question to a parent who grew up constantly hearing negative feedback about their school progress, in particular with mathematics. What do you think the message would be if we communicate with that parent in a negative light about their child? Likely, the parent might start to think that math is a gene and their child will never succeed at math because they didn't either. If we as educators are truly about developing growth mindsets and reversing the once very popular notion that we inherit good or poor math skills, then we must communicate with parents in a way that empowers them to see what their child *can* do.

Four core wants icon sourcse: Helpful by appleuzr/iStock.com; Intelligent by PeterSnow/iStock.com; Confident by Bigmouse108/iStock.com; Familiar by PeterSnow/iStock.com.

Figure 4.5 provides an example of how we can communicate in a strengths-based and specific manner to a parent whose child is struggling with learning two-digit multiplication because they do not *yet* know all their multiplication facts from memory, slowing down the two-digit multiplication process.

Figure 4.5 – Strengths-Based Versus Deficit-Based Math Communication to Parents About Mathematics

Strengths Based and Specific	Deficit Based and Not Specific
[Name of Child] is doing a great job in multiplication using the basic fact fluency they know from memory, such as the 0s, 1s, 2s, 5s, and 10s (e.g., 0 × 1, 2 × 0, 2 × 5, 10 × 2, 5 × 10). Today we played a game that will help them strengthen their memory with the 6s, 7s, 8s, and 9s (e.g., 6 × 8, 9 × 7, 8 × 8). When you play this game at home, notice how they strategically use their 5s fact fluency to help them figure out their 6s, 7s, 8s, and 9s!	[Name of Child] is struggling with remembering their multiplication facts. This is impacting their ability to multiply double-digit numbers. Please spend some time at home reviewing their basic facts.

Notice the difference in the language used in Figure 4.5. We started with something a parent would *want* to read—good news about their child's learning—because everyone has strengths and we want to highlight for the parent the child's strengths. When we wrote about the area where we want to see improvement, we purposefully avoided the word "struggle" or any words that indicate a lack of a skill. We also gave the parent suggestions for additional practice and specified exactly *what* the child needs to practice. Lastly, we intentionally included another strength that we want the parents to notice as they play the game together.

Providing parents with an understanding of where their child should be in that year's mathematics learning trajectory is important. This way, parents can start to see for themselves the progress their child is making, especially if the progress is not exactly where it should be.

Relate to What Parents Know

Have you ever noticed that you remember some things better than others? Much of the new information we learn and retain is because we make associations with previous knowledge or experiences. Jay, Rose, and Simmons (2018) state that "parents are more likely to respond positively to strategies that align with their existing conceptions" (p. 1). Just like the good teaching strategy of activating prior knowledge before teaching new concepts to students, we must set the stage in our communication of new information to parents about the way mathematics is taught today by relating to past knowledge.

One way to do this is to make associations to things with which parents are already familiar. Using the "parentspeak" column in Figure 4.4 as an example, simply adding an extra part that directly connects parents to the way they learned can prove helpful. Look at Figure 4.6 to see what we mean.

Figure 4.6 – Drawing Associations to the Familiar

Why we are learning it this way:

Growing up, you may have added numbers like this:

$$\begin{array}{r} \overset{1}{4}5 \\ +56 \\ \hline 1\ 0\ 1 \end{array}$$

Your child will learn to add numbers like this in fourth grade. We want to make sure they first understand how our number system works so that when they write it like this, they understand *why* they are doing the steps.

Look at how the way we are learning connects to the way they will learn it later:

$$\begin{array}{r} 45 = 40 + 5 \\ + 56 = 50 + 6 \\ \hline 101 = 90 + 11 \end{array} \quad \longleftrightarrow \quad \begin{array}{r} \overset{1}{4}5 \\ +56 \\ \hline 1\ 0\ 1 \end{array}$$

Students add 5 + 6 and 40 + 50 + 10 in both methods, but writing out the numbers by their place values helps students understand *how much the numbers are worth*. This will help prevent mistakes later on when they get to fourth grade and learn a shorter method.

Notice how by adding this content, we have now connected the way we teach math today to the way parents learned math years ago. We also reassured them that their child *will* in fact learn the "old way," too, and described exactly when it will happen so they can expect when to see it. This provides parents an understanding of the mathematics learning trajectory. This type of communication may prevent parents from teaching their child at home the way they learned because they will see that (a) eventually the child will learn that way and (b) there is a reason for not teaching it yet. Ultimately, the more frequently you communicate the *why*, *how*, and *what* and help relate to what parents know, the more parents' four core wants are met.

Just like the good teaching strategy of activating prior knowledge before teaching new concepts to students, we must set the stage in our communication of new information to parents about the way mathematics is taught today by relating to past knowledge.

Communicate Frequently

You might be wondering, "How often does 'frequently' mean?" This is a great question and one that can really only be answered by you and the families with which you communicate. Your relationship with the individual parents *and* information gleaned from surveys (e.g., the attitudinal survey found in the Chapter 1 Apply It! exercise) will help you determine how frequently you will want to communicate.

Most parents want more communication and information. In all of our interviews, we never heard from parents who felt their school overcommunicated about math. In fact, it was quite the opposite. We heard time and time again that parents want more information about the way math is taught today, more direction on how to help at home, and more understanding about where students should be in their trajectory of learning.

HERE ARE A FEW EXAMPLES OF SOME THINGS PARENTS HAVE SAID:

I want more information, there is not too much for me—letters home of just "Hey, here's where math is at in schools these days." We want to know, we're supportive of it, but it's not how we learned.

— Parent of a First Grader

Send more emails with more details. Tell me what I need to know! Just this conversation alone has been so helpful. It's more than I received from the school.

— Parent of Fourth and Fifth Graders

More frequent communication . . . What's the progress? Where should their understanding be? How can I help improve that understanding? And I think that "How can I help?" is the important piece because I think we all want our children to experience success and I think bridging that area through communication would be a big help.

— Parent of a Fifth Grader

To help mitigate the fear of undercommunicating or being perceived as not communicating enough, we suggest asking parents how they prefer communication about math.

Questions You Might Ask

1. What are the best ways to keep you informed about the math we will learn? (Check all that apply.)

   ❏ Email
   ❏ Text message
   ❏ Classroom website
   ❏ Hard copy paper stapled to agenda notebook
   ❏ App (specify the educational technology app you use)
   ❏ Other: _____

2. How often would you like to receive information about the math we are learning and why we are learning in a different way than in the past? (Choose one.)

   ❏ Weekly
   ❏ Twice a month
   ❏ Monthly
   ❏ Once a quarter, trimester, or semester
   ❏ Other: _____

3. How often would you like to receive information on how you can help your child at home with the math we are learning?

   ❏ Weekly
   ❏ Twice a month
   ❏ Monthly
   ❏ Other: _____

These questions can be added to any written correspondence you plan to send to parents. We suggest adding them to a beginning of the year survey (e.g., the one in the Chapter 1 Apply It! exercise) or a beginning of the year letter. In Chapter 5, we will discuss the beginning of the year letter in depth, along with *what* communication looks like schoolwide, classwide, and individually. When thinking about *how* to communicate with parents about mathematics, we also must consider the tools we are using to communicate and when to use which tool.

TOOLS FOR COMMUNICATION AND WHEN TO USE THEM

TIP!

Many different family structures exist, and it is essential that leaders, teachers, and other educators respect the various family make-ups. Be sure that all mathematics communication includes all individuals who have custody of a child (e.g., students who live in more than one home).

When we talk about *how* to communicate, it is necessary to recognize that communication is a two-way street. Simply informing parents with one-sided communication is not enough to move the pendulum. We must ensure that parents have an opportunity to respond to our information so we know they read and understood it and what we must do next to further the learning.

Years ago, teachers and school leaders had few ways of connecting with families other than through in-person conferences, phone calls home, or hard copy assignments and letters shipped via students' backpacks. Today, we are blessed to find ourselves loaded with options, both traditional and technologically enhanced. Now there are many different ways school leaders and teachers communicate with parents, whether via traditional methods (e.g., phone calls or hard copy correspondence) or digital methods (e.g., emails, texts, applications, or websites). No matter which tools you use to communicate, it is pivotal to recognize when it is best to use which tool and to ensure there is a two-way system built so parents can respond to the information provided.

Traditional Communication

There are many ways to communicate with families without making use of technology, or what we call "traditional communication." These types of communication are phone calls and hard copy correspondence that tends to go home through a student's backpack.

Phone Calls

The old "phone call home" goes a long way, especially in today's society where socializing often occurs through a written or digital platform. Phone calls are a quick and easy way to ensure two-way communication, and they are a great tool for building and maintaining relationships with parents.

In one study, Kraft and Dougherty (2013) found that "improved teacher–student relationships are facilitated by frequent, proactive calls made by teachers rather than reactive calls that focus on problems in the classroom" (p. 199). The authors note that having schoolwide consistency in place, such as providing teachers with a minimum expectation about call frequency and call content, would help ensure that phone calls home actually take place. If you teach in a school without schoolwide structures in place to support this, consider creating a schedule of frequency so that each parent receives a certain number of phone calls home (in particular about mathematics) per year.

We suggest using a phone call to open the lines of communication and share positive news about the child's math learning. Given that many adults fear mathematics, hearing something positive may help put them at ease. For teachers, consider calling parents between the second to fourth week of school to introduce yourself and share some positive information about the child's math learning. Using strengths-based language will model for the parent high expectations and how to praise effort and process. Look at Figure 4.7 to see some examples of how you can use general mathematical habits and behaviors (like those in the Standards for Mathematical Practice or Process Standards; National Governors Association Center for Best Practices, Council of Chief State School Officers, 2010) that we hope to see students exhibit to guide your conversations.

Be sure to document all phone calls home in a log—even positive phone calls. We suggest keeping a log that shows the date of the call, time, with whom, purpose of call, and brief comments about the exchange. Here is an example of documentation of one phone call. The next phone call would be listed directly under the first entry.

Date	Time	Spoke To	Purpose of Call	Comments
9/10/2019	3:30–3:43 p.m.	Nadia Valencia, mother of Ana	Introductory call home; I called her.	She didn't know about the classroom website, so I let her know how to access it. I also told her how Ana has been brave during math class by explaining her thinking and asked her to share how proud she is with Ana about that.

Figure 4.7 – Example of Mathematics Phone Calls Home

Example Mathematical Habits	Examples of What You Could Say
Persevering	• "I was really impressed today when [Name of Student] took their time through a really challenging task that on other days they might have given up on. Will you let them know you are proud of them for persevering through a challenging task?" • "I was so proud that I had to call and share with you this moment of success for [Name of Student] during math class. We were working on a pretty challenging word problem and initially, they got frustrated and needed a break, but then came back and said, 'I'll try again' and was able to show their thinking. They showed true perseverance."
Making Sense of a Task	• "I wanted to tell you about how proud I was today when [Name of Student] made sense of a math task we were working on. They must have listened closely when we taught about how to be a problem-solver because they followed the steps perfectly. First they read the problem. Then, they asked themself what the story is about and were able to retell the story. They rephrased what the question was asking and ultimately used what information was given to be able to solve in a way that made sense for them."
Attending to Precision	• "Today was such a successful day for [Name of Student] in math class. As you know, we have been working on our accuracy and today they found an error on their own and were able to figure out how to fix it without any support. They were very proud of themselves, and so I hope you can share at home how proud you are that they were paying attention to their accuracy during math."
Using Tools Strategically	• "I had to share with you about how [Name of Student] used math to help another student today. We did not have enough rulers for everyone, so they offered to give their ruler to someone else and strategically used a piece of paper as a straightedge. If you want to praise them at home, I suggest sharing that you are glad they acted kindly and that they were able to use math to solve a real-life problem!"
Constructing Mathematical Argument and Critiquing Others	• "I am calling to tell you about how [Name of Student] has done an incredible job this week explaining their thinking and helping others to understand how they solve problems. I think it would help them communicate with others more if you also share with them that you are proud that they are justifying their thinking," • "I wanted to let you know that [Name of Student] did an incredible job today disagreeing with someone in a respectful way and helping the class to see a different perspective. It was brave! Do you mind reinforcing at home that you are proud that they were able to help others see a different way of thinking in a kind manner?"

Example Mathematical Habits	Examples of What You Could Say
Self-Identifying as a Mathematical Thinker	• "I wanted to tell you that over the course of the past few weeks, [Name of Student] has started to really own their place as a mathematician in our classroom. In the beginning of the year, they were shy to share their thinking in front of others, but lately they have been saying things like, 'I am not sure if I am correct, but I know mathematicians make lots of mistakes before they get to the right answer.'"
	• "I just wanted to let you know how impressed I am that [Name of Student] took the work we are doing in math class and during art class today noticed patterns and helped others see that art includes math. I wonder if you could also praise them for thinking like a mathematician?"

Phone calls are a great way to build personal relationships with parents and to touch base about timely information that is better said orally than through writing.

Hard Copy Correspondence

Another way to correspond with parents is via paper. Hard copy correspondence generally refers to all the papers that go home with the child. Examples of hard copy correspondence include classwide letters, such as beginning of the year letters, unit preview letters, weekly letters, and surveys, as well as all the student's work. All hard copy correspondence can also be sent via digital methods, but many parents still like to receive some sort of hard copy information, especially if access is an issue.

Most elementary students have agenda books to help them organize and record their homework and assignments. One tactic many teachers use to help engage parents is requiring that a parent sign the agenda notebook each night, with the hope that this means the parent has checked the homework and read what is written. Though well intentioned, what often happens is that busy parents sign for the sake of signing without looking at anything. Daily signatures can become burdensome for parents and can create anxiety for students whose parents forgot or missed it.

Instead, teachers can try requesting weekly signatures attached to a more focused task. For example, teachers can create an insert (such as

> **TIP!**
>
> Parents do not need to know the language of the Standards for Mathematical Practice or any other process standards. Instead, they should have an understanding of general habits of mathematical thinkers. This might mean changing the writing style of the practices or processes from eduspeak to parentspeak.

> **TIP!**
>
> Consider sending hard copy correspondence with a footer note (when appropriate) stating that this correspondence has also been sent via another communication method, such as email or a specific digital tool. This will help parents know which paper copies they can access in other places or if this is the only copy they have.

Figure 4.8) that gets stapled into the students' agenda notebooks weekly with an expectation for signature by the following week. This will help keep the parents informed, reiterate what was already sent in either a weekly or unit preview letter, and help parents see their child's progress for themselves. Read Chapter 5 to see how to write this type of communication and alternative ways to use it.

Figure 4.8 – Agenda Notebook Insert

Dear Families,

This week your child learned to add numbers between 10 and 99 using **partial sums**. You can help your child at home by asking them to show you how to find the total for 39 + 57 using this strategy. If they struggle, ask these questions:

- Do you think the answer will be greater or less than 100? Why?
- How can you rewrite 39 as tens and ones?
- How can you rewrite 57 as tens and ones?
- What do you get when you add the tens and the tens? The ones and the ones?
- Can you draw your base-ten blocks to help you?

Families, please check one and sign below by Monday.

☐   I asked my child and they taught me the strategy successfully.

☐   I asked my child and they needed me to ask some of the questions provided, but they eventually got it.

☐   I asked my child, but they struggled. Please let me know what else I can do to help.

☐   I did not ask, but will soon.

Signature

X _____

TIP!

When sending home hard copy assignments or letters, staple them to the current weekly page in the child's agenda notebook. This will prevent the papers from getting lost at the bottom of the backpack.

Beyond the traditional forms of communication, using digital tools to communicate with parents is ever more popular these days and a great way to get information to parents who can access it.

Digital Communication

Two-way communication can also be enhanced with technology. According to the most recent report from the U.S. Census Bureau (2018a), 92% of households had access to some type of device that could connect to the Internet. In addition, 88% of households had Internet access (U.S. Census Bureau, 2018b). Another report from Pew Research Center (2019) shows that 81% of adults also own a smartphone. Given these data, educators can make intentional decisions on how best to use digital tools to communicate. Ultimately, the best way to know which methods of communication about mathematics work best for parents is to survey them, using questions such as the ones provided earlier in this chapter.

There are three other main platforms that teachers and school leaders use for communication about mathematics beyond the traditional phone calls and hard copy correspondence. These are websites, educational technology applications, and email. Let us explore how we can best make use of these for communicating with parents about mathematics.

District and School Websites

Websites are one of the best tools we can use as educators to keep parents informed about their child's general mathematics education. Websites work best when they act as landing pages and resource sites for parents to peruse at their own convenience. There are two levels of websites that parents must navigate: district/school websites and classroom websites.

District and school websites should offer the most information relative to school/districtwide agreements around mathematics teaching and learning. Schools and districts that generally do not have consistency in beliefs or structure often have websites that are missing crucial information. This is why school leaders must work with their teachers to develop structures that enable consistency, as discussed in Chapter 3. Once these structures are in place, school and district websites can be resourceful and informative tools for parents.

At a minimum, we believe a well-organized district or school website should make the following information easily accessible for parents:

- Shared mathematics vision or belief statement about what mathematics teaching and learning looks like in this community;
- Links to identified or adopted curricular resources;
- List of mathematics content standards in parent-friendly language, explicitly showing what children should know and be able to do by the end of the school year at each grade level;
- Description of roles and responsibilities of families in their child's mathematics learning journey, inclusive of homework expectations;

> **TIP!**
>
> The National Council of Teachers of Mathematics (NCTM) and the Hunt Institute (2015) have produced a video series for parents, which schools and districts can embed on their websites as placeholders until they have their own videos showcasing their own teachers, students, and methods. See https://hunt-institute. org/resources/2015/04/ nctm-mathematics-video-series-parents-supporting-mathematics-learning/. Be sure to provide a short annotated description of what each video is about to help set the stage for parents. Also provide captions in native languages relative to your school or district context.

- Components of a typical mathematics block or lesson so parents can visualize or see what 21st century learning looks like; and
- Access to resources such as videos, games, and supports.

Howard County Public School System (HCPSS), located in Maryland, is one example of a school district that has a mathematics-focused, spotlight-worthy districtwide website for families. Starting from the main district site, a parent can quickly understand the beliefs and position that HCPSS holds for its students. Additionally, HCPSS has a specific site designed just for families. They call it the HCPSS Mathematics Support Center and it is easily accessible via the main district mathematics site.

The HCPSS Mathematics Support Center is structured around three goals that center on helping families:

1. Gain a better understanding of their child's math program;
2. Refresh or build deeper understanding of math concepts, skills, and practices; and
3. Provide additional support and practice opportunities for students, including free online homework help as needed, throughout the school year.

These goals are clearly visible for parents to see and the site is easy to navigate. Parents can select from a variety of options, including clicking on their child's grade level to find an abundance of support. Examples of resources include an overview of content standards that will be covered in the school year, a year-at-a-glance map that shows exactly when the standards will be covered, definitions of mathematics vocabulary, resources for particular content areas, and much more.

CHECK IT OUT FOR YOURSELF!

- HCPSS District Mathematics site: https://www.hcpss.org/academics/mathematics/
- HCPSS Mathematics Support Center: https://hcpssfamilymath.weebly.com

---

While a well-organized school/district website is a good resource for parents, teachers often have little to no control as to whether those sites exist and are updated. This is where a classroom website becomes critical.

Classroom Websites

Like school and district websites, classroom websites act as trusted resources for parents. A classroom website is a great place to house important information that was previously communicated to parents and could easily get lost in a backpack or inbox. The classroom website gives parents a safe place to turn when they need help or are looking for something specific. For example, posting daily or weekly homework assignments on a classroom website is a great way to communicate with families about what is expected to be done at home. When students forget to write down the assignment in their agenda notebooks or they cannot read what they wrote during class, there is a resource available to help guide them and their parents at home.

If your school or district has a well-stocked mathematics site, then the classroom website can simply reiterate the information on the main site by linking to important documents. If your school or district does not yet have a detailed family-oriented mathematics site, then consider providing the needed information on a classroom website.

A classroom website is helpful to parents when it does the following:

- Links to important documents on the school/district mathematics site,
- Reiterates schoolwide norms around math (if none exist, it then highlights the classroom norms about math; e.g., mistakes are learning opportunities),
- States the parent's role in their child's math learning,
- States homework expectations and assignments,
- Offers resources, such as videos or games to support the content, and
- Identifies the best ways for parents to contact you.

In addition to or in place of classroom websites, many schools and classrooms use educational technology applications to enhance communication.

Educational Technology Applications

Educational technology applications, or Edtech apps, have transformed education as we know it. These device-friendly tools have enabled teachers, school leaders, and parents to engage in more learning and communication than ever before. Examples of commonly used Edtech apps are Remind, Seesaw, Edmodo, and ParentSquare. Using any of the available Edtech apps is a great way to enhance your communication with families.

In particular, these apps are great for acting as windows into the classroom. Use Edtech apps to provide your parents frequent, positive, and informed communication through video of their children actively learning. There is nothing a parent loves more than to see their child happy. This is powerful because it enables parents to see what actually happens in classrooms. By doing this, parents can start to

1. See that math is fun and joyful,
2. Observe math tools that are used in the classroom,
3. Look at strategies being used to enhance student understanding, and
4. Communicate with their child about the math they are doing.

Consider capturing a short video of a child justifying their thinking to a peer and share that video with the parent through the app with a caption like this: "[Name of Student] justifying their thinking in math class to a partner. Please praise them at home for explaining their thinking so others can learn!" You can also take a picture of a student's work and send that immediately to a parent to help them see what their child is learning in class. Similarly, parents can respond by sharing texts, pictures, or videos from home as well, sometimes helping teachers see how parents are building on the work done during the school day.

Edtech apps also act as communication platforms, often looking a lot like emails or text messages. You can send whole-class messages as well as individual parent messages. Depending on the platform chosen, lots of features (e.g., notifications, read receipts, and more) can elevate parent involvement. Apps that allow you to check read receipts offer helpful benefits. For example, they help you use data to inform your next move (e.g., 98% of the families opened the message you sent. Check to see the 2% that didn't. How could you connect with them?), and they provide you a little more information than email or hardcopy notes because you usually cannot see whether those messages have been read or opened.

Apps also provide a storage place for your communication. Many of the commonly used Edtech apps have folders where you can keep past and ongoing communication with individual parents. Unlike text messaging, this provides a level of ease for the parent who can go back and reference if needed, and it also provides you a documentation log.

An important reminder about apps has to do with consistency of choice in which ones are used. In our interviews with parents and educators, we heard about 25 different communication platforms being used across educators. Further, some interviews showcased at least five different platforms used within the same school district or school. For parents of twins, triplets, or even children of different ages, imagine how stressful it must be to use one app for one child's class and another app for another child's class. There should not be 30 different teachers using 30 different platforms for communication, unless some teachers are piloting a different app for possible schoolwide adoption. This is why the schoolwide structures we discussed in Chapter 3 need to be in place. For this reason, we advise teachers to consult with peers and leadership in their school before they implement any new modes of communication on their own.

> **There should not be 30 different teachers using 30 different platforms for communication.**

Tips If There Is No Schoolwide Policy on Apps

If your school has not set schoolwide expectations yet about which apps to use, consider starting with your grade-level team for consensus. Consider equity and access before determining which app you will use. For example, depending on your families' access, you may want to choose apps that do not require a smartphone. It also might be best to choose platforms that use text messaging and do not require an Internet connection. Keep in mind that some cell phone plans charge per text message, so it is good practice to survey parents to find out the best ways to communicate before initiating app use. You also might want to consider an app that translates messages for you into other languages. Because language differences can be a barrier, apps like this can ease communication. (Here are some suggestions: TalkingPoints, Remind, Seesaw, ParentSquare, SimplyCircle, BuzzMob, Appletree, Bloomz, and Class Messenger, among others.)

Email

Email is another digital way to communicate with families. Many Edtech apps incorporate email and text messaging, so this section may not seem applicable to those who use Edtech apps religiously. However, if you do not use Edtech apps, then email might be one way in which you communicate with families. Email can be used very similarly to Edtech apps and phone calls home. You can send a quick note to a parent via email with a picture of student work or a child engaging in learning, along with a strengths-based message like those suggested in Figure 4.7. Or you can simply write a short note, best used proactively, to reinforce a mathematical behavior that you would like to continue to see.

Resources About Tools for Communicating With Parents

JOURNAL ARTICLE

"Using Mobile Technologies to Communicate With Parents and Caregivers" by A. N. Gauvreau and S. R. Sandall (2019), published in *Young Exceptional Children*

BOOK

New Ways to Engage Parents: Strategies and Tools for Teachers and Leaders, K–12 by Patricia Edwards and Catherine Compton-Lilly (2016)

PUTTING IT ALL TOGETHER

In this chapter, we explored *how* to communicate with parents about mathematics by looking at what makes communication with parents effective and thinking critically about various modes of communication. Equally as critical as knowing *how* to communicate is also knowing *what* to communicate at a more specific and granular level to meet parents' wishes and needs and attend to parents' four core wants. In Chapter 5, we will look at *what* to communicate through three levels of communication (school, classroom, and individual) and discuss various ways to enhance written communication about mathematics.

FREQUENTLY ASKED QUESTIONS

Q How can I assess parents' understanding of the communication that I send home? Essentially, how will I know that what I am doing is effective?

A It is difficult to determine the effectiveness of communication with parents. Sometimes, there is also a disconnect between what teachers are communicating and what parents understand and interpret. One suggestion is to conduct a survey periodically to assess whether parents perceive the modes and quality of communication to be effective. The benefits of online tools for communication generally are that you can see who has opened the correspondence and the two-way platform is easily built into the programs. Hard copy correspondence is more challenging because there is no "read receipt." Establishing formative check-ins like you do with students could help. For example, after you send home a unit preview letter, ask parents to respond to the correspondence by sharing one challenge they are having and give them an option for not experiencing a challenge at this time. Just as we give formative and summative assessments to students, we can do the same with parents.

Q I only have time to make phone calls when I need to report an infraction made by a student. How can I make time to make calls home about other things?

A Making phone calls home certainly is an investment of time compared to other modes of correspondence. As we stated in this chapter, focusing more on strengths-based communication can help you improve your teacher–parent relationships. Building relationships is a key part of teacher–parent communication. Creating a schedule might help limit the time it takes. For example, aim to call five parents per week, spread out over the week, and strategically plan the calls so they are no more than 10 minutes. Alternatively, you can also work with your administration to see if the last 10 minutes of the school day can be dedicated to parent communication.

Q It seems that new technologies for educators are being created so fast. If I see a new application midway through the year, can I try and use it with families?

A There is no doubt that technological advances move at a rapid pace. Although there might be an urge to switch to the newest mode of communication via a new app, it is important to slow down. If you and your team or school decided on a particular mode for the school year, then stick with it. If you hear of something new that has come out, consider learning it and sharing with colleagues for implementation for the following school year. It may cause more stress than good for you and parents to implement a new mode of communication mid-year.

APPLY IT! TEACHER ACTIVITIES

How Will You Improve *How* You Communicate?

1. Take a look back at all the suggestions we provided in this chapter. What is one strategy you have yet to try? Take some time and try it out.

2. Consider the importance of using parent surveys to specifically elicit feedback about which modes of communication they prefer and how often they prefer to receive general mathematics communication and communication about their child's progress.

    a. What questions will help you determine which tools or modes to use?

    b. What will you need to do to prepare for frequent communication if that is what parents ask for?

    c. What will you do if your classroom of parents are split on their responses? How will you decide which modes to use and the frequency?

APPLY IT! SCHOOL LEADER ACTIVITIES

How Will You Improve *How* You Communicate?

1. Take a look back at all the suggestions we provided in this chapter. Which of them do you find most important for your teachers to do? Choose one that you want to ensure all teachers are implementing. Develop an action plan to help the teachers put the work in place. Consider the following:

   a. What structures need to be in place for this to work?

   b. What barriers to success might exist?

   c. What resources can you provide your staff to make this happen?

2. Think about the various modes of communication used by your staff. Make a tally chart outlining all the modes. Reflect on the following:

   a. How many different modes exist in the building?

   b. Are there multiple educational technology apps being utilized? If so, how can you reduce the number?

   c. How can you work toward schoolwide consistency?

CHAPTER 5

Exploring *What* to Communicate to Parents About Math

*The quality of your communication determines
the size of your result.*

— Meir Ezra

IN THIS CHAPTER YOU WILL . . .

- Look at written communication from three different levels (school, classroom, and student),
- Reflect on *what* you communicate mathematically to parents and how to do it proactively, and
- Think critically about how to use the data from two-way communication to improve the delivery of information to parents.

As you read in Chapter 4, knowing *how* to communicate with parents is key to ensuring that they are equipped to receive the information sent their way. Knowing *what* to communicate is equally as critical. If the *what* does not match the needs, then it won't matter *how* it's communicated. In this chapter, we offer specific ways for teachers and school leaders to connect the *what* to the *how* of communication.

We believe there are three levels of communication:

1. Parents at large (school level)
2. Parents as a class (classroom level)
3. Parents as individuals (student level)

All three levels should be readable, accessible, proactive, strengths based, and two way in their

Icon source: Momento Design/iStock.com.

nature. As you read this chapter, pay attention to the ways in which we suggest leveraging one-way communication so it becomes two-way communication. It is important to note that frequency in communication among these three levels will vary. Let's take a deeper look into the three levels.

REACHING PARENTS AT LARGE

Generally, administrators are responsible for communicating to parents at large. Because the information needs to be accessible for all grade levels, usually this type of communication is more high level and provides overviews and expectations. More specific communication would come at the classroom level. Examples of communication that might go out at a school level are a beginning of the year letter focused on schoolwide math norms and expectations, schoolwide math homework expectations and grading information (as discussed in Chapter 3), and a mid- or end-of-year homework survey.

Schoolwide Beginning of the Year Letter

A schoolwide beginning of the year letter helps set the foundation for the norms and expectations around mathematics teaching and learning. Often administrators are responsible for this type of communication. This letter is important because it sets the schoolwide tone and can act as an artifact that teachers can revisit if they are struggling with parental involvement. Often schoolwide communication pertains to more than just mathematics, so consider how this message will be sent. Will it be part of a larger beginning of the year letter or will it stand on its own? Figure 5.1 offers an excerpt that can be included within a larger letter that might be used at the beginning of the year to communicate these schoolwide mathematical expectations. If you are a teacher in a school where you do not have schoolwide consensus, consider integrating the excerpt as part of your own classroom beginning of the year letter.

TIP!

Make this beginning of the year correspondence two-way communication by turning it into a parent–school contract or pact. Add a section where parents check off that they have read and agree to the "terms" of the school, and provide a place for questions. Teachers can collect the "agreements" and questions as evidence that the document was read. Keep these for the duration of the school year in case anyone needs to refer back to what parents agreed to later on!

Figure 5.1

Example Excerpt From a Beginning of the Year Letter

 [Explain the school's approach to teaching math.]

We at [Name of School] are excited to start teaching and learning math! We are using a balanced approach that includes teaching math for deep understanding, engaging in problem-solving, and solidifying skills in carrying out procedures flexibly, accurately, efficiently, and appropriately. Our goal is to ensure every student is given the opportunity to engage in meaningful, rigorous mathematics. With your support, all children will see themselves as mathematical thinkers.

 [Explain the top three facts we suggest about today's math.]

The way we teach math today may be different than how you learned it. Here's why:

1. **Math instruction, like technology, medicine, and more, is always evolving.** Many adults grew up hating math because of the way it was taught. As a result, some adults avoided specific careers that use math explicitly. Research has shown that by changing how we teach math, more people can understand it and grow a love for it.

2. **We also value understanding more than someone's ability to calculate and get answers quickly because math is not genetic.** This means you will see us praising your child's process, effort, and different strategies instead of their answers and intellect.

3. **The math your child is learning today is meant to set them up for their future.** This is why you will see your child thinking critically, collaborating, and communicating more in math than ever before.

Remember, everyone is a mathematical thinker. For more on this, here is a short, 3-minute YouTube video you might find helpful on today's math: "The Top 3 Facts Every Parent Needs to Know About Today's Math" (https://bit.ly/AddingParents).

 [Introduce math norms for your building and state expectations for parents to use them at home.]

As a school, we have established some essential math norms. Math norms are expectations our school has for all math learners. These norms help us create a math community where we can feel safe asking questions, making mistakes, and using different strategies to solve problems. We ask you to help us build these math norms by also establishing them in your home.

Four core wants icon sources: Confident by Bigmouse108/iStock.com; Intelligent by PeterSnow/iStock.com; Familiar by PeterSnow/iStock.com.

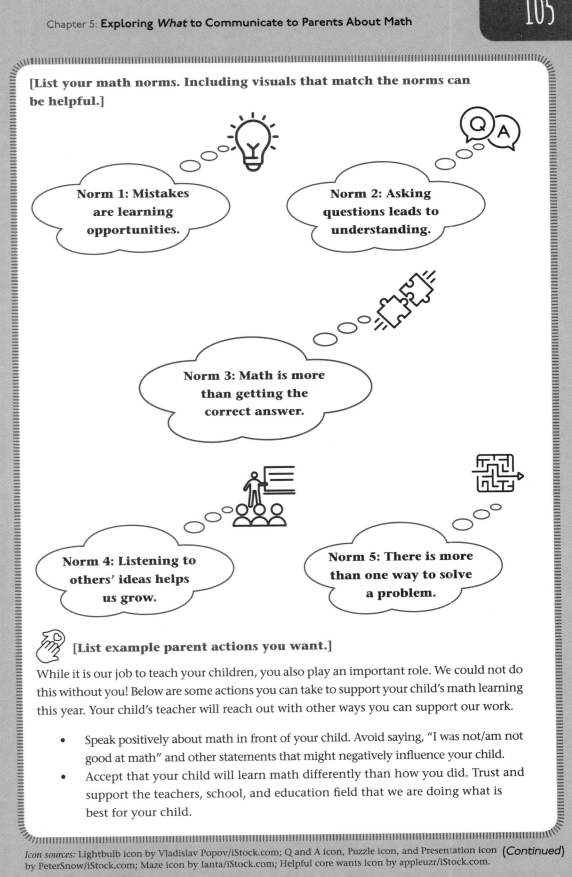

[List your math norms. Including visuals that match the norms can be helpful.]

Norm 1: Mistakes are learning opportunities.

Norm 2: Asking questions leads to understanding.

Norm 3: Math is more than getting the correct answer.

Norm 4: Listening to others' ideas helps us grow.

Norm 5: There is more than one way to solve a problem.

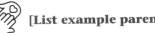 [List example parent actions you want.]

While it is our job to teach your children, you also play an important role. We could not do this without you! Below are some actions you can take to support your child's math learning this year. Your child's teacher will reach out with other ways you can support our work.

- Speak positively about math in front of your child. Avoid saying, "I was not/am not good at math" and other statements that might negatively influence your child.
- Accept that your child will learn math differently than how you did. Trust and support the teachers, school, and education field that we are doing what is best for your child.

Icon sources: Lightbulb icon by Vladislav Popov/iStock.com; Q and A icon, Puzzle icon, and Presentation icon *(Continued)* by PeterSnow/iStock.com; Maze icon by Ianta/iStock.com; Helpful core wants icon by appleuzr/iStock.com.

(*Continued*)

- Allow your child to struggle. To learn how to problem-solve, struggle is necessary.
- Encourage your child to ask questions and be curious about math.
- Be a learner with your child. Ask them about what they are learning and to teach you their strategies.
- Reinforce the strategies your child learns in school. Reach out to your child's teacher if you don't understand so they can support you.

  Available for download at **resources.corwin.com/partneringwithparents/elementary**

Homework Communication From the School to Parents

> **TIP!**
>
> If you are a teacher in a school where this type of correspondence will not be sent from the school level, consider sending relevant parts from you and/or your grade-level team.

School-level communication around homework can be done via the beginning of the year letter, the school student/parent handbook, or a standalone letter. In the beginning of the year, parents receive a lot of information. We suggest embedding this information in another piece of correspondence to minimize the number of letters they receive. Look at Figure 5.2 for an example excerpt of school to parent homework communication.

Figure 5.2

Example Excerpt of Math Homework Expectations

At [Name of School], we value opportunities for independent practice and review of content taught during the school day. We view math homework as an opportunity to enhance understanding, not as a place to assign new content that has yet to be taught. You should expect to see homework that helps students practice a particular skill they have learned or apply skills they have learned to a problem-solving task. Homework will be assigned daily in Grades 3–5 and weekly in Grades K–2. Refer to the following chart to see how long daily math homework should take at each grade level. If you find your child taking 5 minutes or more than the time listed, please contact your child's teacher.

Grade Level	Approximate Amount of Daily Math Homework
Kindergarten	5 minutes
Grades 1 and 2	10 minutes
Grades 3 and 4	15 minutes
Grade 5	20 minutes

Homework helps teachers understand areas of struggle and gives them information about how to adjust their teaching to meet the needs of the students. A common parent misunderstanding is that teachers want to see homework completed and done correctly. When parents do the homework with (and sometimes for) the child, teachers then cannot see where help is needed. For this reason, we ask parents to play a specific role when it comes to homework. Look at the following chart to see what we expect of our students, parents, and teachers with regard to homework. Please reach out to your child's teacher if you have specific questions about the roles.

Student, Parent, and Teacher Roles With Homework		
Students	**Parents**	**Teachers**
• Know what the assignments are • Complete assignments on time • Put forth best effort • Let the teacher know if they do not understand an assignment or will have difficulty completing it on time	As best as they can . . . • Know what the assignments are • Provide their child a safe and quiet work space • Convey a positive attitude in front of their child about math and school • Establish clear homework routines • Provide guidance, not answers • Watch for signs of frustration and provide breaks • Allow their child to hand in an incomplete assignment • Help the child write a note to the teacher letting them know exactly what the child does not understand or asking for more time to complete it	• Assign high-quality assignments that fall within the school's policy, differentiating as needed • Ensure homework is written in agenda notebooks and/or on the class website • State the purpose of the assignment for parents and students • Provide clear directions and exemplars, where applicable • Clarify what students need to do to demonstrate that the assignment has been completed • Review homework in a timely manner and provide feedback • Contact parents if homework is not received

online resources Available for download at **resources.corwin.com/partneringwithparents/elementary**

Turn this homework letter into a two-way communication by making it a contract between the student, parent, and teacher/school! Add a section to the roles chart where students and parents sign that they have read the expectations for homework and understand their roles. Here's an example:

Student Name:	Parent Name:	Teacher Name:
Student Signature:	Parent Signature:	Teacher Signature:
I understand my role as a student.	I understand my role as a parent.	I understand my role as a teacher.

Keep these letters for the duration of the school year in case you need to refer back to what students and parents agreed to later on.

Mid-Year Homework Survey

Beginning of the year correspondence is critical to establishing proactive and positive communication, but parents also want to receive ongoing communication.

The examples shown so far have focused on beginning of the year correspondence. Beginning of the year correspondence is critical to establishing proactive and positive communication, but parents also want to receive ongoing communication. While communication will happen more frequently at the classroom and individual levels, ongoing schoolwide communication can serve a larger purpose. Conducting a mid- and/or end-of-year survey can help you gather data and use them to improve on the norms and expectations that were initially set.

By mid-year, parents have already received school- and classroom-level communication about math homework, so surveying schoolwide about actual experiences can help the school improve its work (Figure 5.3). This is a great way to understand from families if the amount of time spent on homework is too much, too little, or just right and to gauge their perceived quality of assignments. The data collected can be used to adjust practices. Be sure to ask the parent to state the child's grade level so if there are obvious issues, the follow-up work can be directed and focused.

Figure 5.3

Mid-Year Homework Survey

Dear Families,

Please take 2–5 minutes to fill out this survey. Please fill out a new survey for **each** child. Your answers will help us understand how to improve the math homework experience across the school.

1. In what grade level is your child?
   - ❏ Kindergarten
   - ❏ First grade
   - ❏ Second grade
   - ❏ Third grade
   - ❏ Fourth grade
   - ❏ Fifth grade

   At the beginning of the school year, we sent home a letter with this chart:

Grade Level	Approximate Amount of Daily Math Homework
Kindergarten	5 minutes
Grades 1 and 2	10 minutes
Grades 3 and 4	15 minutes
Grade 5	20 minutes

2. Has the amount of daily or weekly homework for math matched our intent?
   - ❏ Always
   - ❏ Mostly
   - ❏ Sometimes
   - ❏ Rarely
   - ❏ Never
   - ❏ I don't know

3. On average, the math homework my child receives:
   - ❏ Is too difficult for my child
   - ❏ Is just right for my child
   - ❏ Is too easy for my child
   - ❏ I don't know

(Continued)

(Continued)

4. On average, the math homework my child receives:
   ❑ Is more than enough
   ❑ Is just the right amount
   ❑ Is not enough
   ❑ I don't know
5. On average, the math homework my child receives:
   ❑ Is useful for my child
   ❑ Is not useful for my child
   ❑ I don't know

Additional Comments:

online resources ⟋ Available for download at **resources.corwin.com/partneringwithparents/elementary**

TIP!

If you are a teacher working in a school that does not plan to use this survey at the schoolwide level, consider using it for your classroom instead. It will give you good feedback as to whether or not what you are assigning is meeting the needs of your families. Use Google Forms or another online form tool for the easiest data collection and the ability to look for overall patterns among the data.

REACHING PARENTS AS A CLASS

Correspondence that does not come from the school leader to parents at large generally comes from the classroom teacher. This type of communication is done in a whole-class manner in which every parent of a child in the classroom receives the same information, even if each teacher tailors it to their own voice and style. While this is done on a classroom-by-classroom basis, it is best if there is consistency horizontally (by members of the same grade level) and even better vertically (by all teachers regardless of grade level), as we described in Chapter 3 with regard to structures. This allows for routine and predictability for parents, leaving the majority of focus to the content that changes year to year instead of routines, content, and more. In this section, we will outline a beginning of the year survey, a beginning of the year letter, unit preview letters, weekly letters, and mid- and end-of-year surveys.

Beginning of the Year Survey

Surveys are a great two-way communication tool because they require parents to do some action and then return them to the school. In the Chapter 1 Apply It! exercise, we shared a sample survey that could be sent home at the beginning of the year. Let's look at two survey results from real parents (Figure 5.4) and see how you could use that data to inform your instruction.

Figure 5.4 – Beginning of the Year Survey Results

SURVEY 1

About YOU

1. The following describes your school life *when you were a child.* (Select all that apply.)

    - ☑ I received formal schooling in the United States.
    - ☐ I received formal schooling outside of the United States.
    - ☐ I was homeschooled.
    - ☐ I did not receive formal schooling.
    - ☐ I prefer not to say.

2. The following best describes your attitude toward math *when you were a child.* (Choose one.)

    - ☐ Loved it!
    - ☐ Liked it.
    - ☑ Didn't love it, but didn't hate it.
    - ☐ Hated it!
    - ☐ Can't remember.

    Comments (if any):

(Continued)

(Continued)

3. The following best describes your attitude toward math *now as an adult*. (Choose one.)

    ☐ Love it!

    ☐ Like it.

    ☐ Don't love it, but don't hate it.

    ☑ Hate it!

    > If there was a change, what caused it?
    >
    > *Having to help my kids with school and not understanding the new ways of teaching it*

4. Check all the statements that are **true** for you.

    ☐ I feel familiar and confident with the way math is taught today.

    ☐ I am excited to learn new ways of looking at and thinking about math.

    ☑ I am nervous. I will confuse my child if I try to help them.

    ☑ I don't understand how math is being taught today.

    ☐ I don't understand why math is being taught differently than the way I learned it.

About YOUR CHILD

1. The following best describes *your child's* attitude toward math. (Choose one.)

    ☐ Loves it!

    ☑ Likes it.

    ☐ Doesn't love it, but doesn't hate it.

☐ Hates it!

☐ I don't know because they never talk about it.

Comments (if any):

2. How do you support your child's understanding of math? (Check all that apply.)

☐ I read books about math with my child often.

☐ We play games and puzzles that involve math.

☑ We do flashcards and help them memorize their facts by repetition.

☐ We do fact review but through games.

☐ I ask my child to show and explain to me what they learn each day.

☐ We find math in everyday life and talk about it.

☑ I help them with their homework.

☐ Other: _____

3. What information do you feel you need about the math your child will learn this year?

Basic introduction instructional videos

4. What else do you think I should know that will help me understand how to support you and your child's math learning this year?

Flashcards

SURVEY 2

About YOU

1. The following describes your school life *when you were a child*. (Select all that apply.)

   [✓] I received formal schooling in the United States.

   [ ] I received formal schooling outside of the United States.

   [ ] I was homeschooled.

   [ ] I did not receive formal schooling.

   [ ] I prefer not to say.

2. The following best describes your attitude toward math *when you were a child*. (Choose one.)

   [ ] Loved it!

   [ ] Liked it.

   [ ] Didn't love it, but didn't hate it.

   [✓] Hated it!

   [ ] Can't remember.

   > Comments (if any):
   >
   > *It was the one subject for which I had very little confidence in my abilities.*

3. The following best describes your attitude toward math *now as an adult*. (Choose one.)

   [ ] Love it!

   [ ] Like it.

   [✓] Don't love it, but don't hate it.

   [ ] Hate it!

If there was a change, what caused it?

The availability of technology that lets me check my answer!

4. Check all the statements that are **true** for you.

☐ I feel familiar and confident with the way math is taught today.

☐ I am excited to learn new ways of looking at and thinking about math.

☑ I am nervous I will confuse my child if I try to help them.

☐ I don't understand how math is being taught today.

☐ I don't understand why math is being taught differently than the way I learned it.

About YOUR CHILD

1. The following best describes *your child's* attitude toward math. (Choose one.)

☑ Loves it!

☐ Likes it.

☐ Doesn't love it, but doesn't hate it.

☐ Hates it!

☐ I don't know because they never talk about it.

Comments (if any):

(Continued)

(Continued)

2. How do you support your child's understanding of math? (Check all that apply.)

☐ I read books about math with my child often.

☑ We play games and puzzles that involve math.

☐ We do flashcards and help them memorize their facts by repetition.

☑ We do fact review but through games.

☐ I ask my child to show and explain to me what they learn each day.

☐ We find math in everyday life and talk about it.

☑ I help them with their homework.

☐ Other: _____

3. What information do you feel you need about the math your child will learn this year?

> *The correct methods being taught since they often differ from what I was taught.*

4. What else do you think I should know that will help me understand how to support you and your child's math learning this year?

> *I would appreciate more communication on the techniques currently taught and theories behind them.*

Looking at Figure 5.4, it is easy to see that with just a few questions, you can gain so much insight into parents' attitudes toward math, their perspective of their child's math work, how they are feeling about the changes in today's math teaching, and how they are supporting their child at home. Take a moment and think about what you learn about the first parent from Survey 1. Then, think about what you learn about the second parent from Survey 2. To help you reflect, complete the following table by writing down what you notice about each survey.

Reflect

Survey 1	Survey 2

When you are finished reflecting, look at our noticings in Figure 5.5. Did you notice the same things? What do these noticings tell you and how can you use the surveys to inform your future communication with these parents?

Reflect icon source: Vladislav Popov/iStock.com.

Figure 5.5 – Survey 1 and Survey 2 Reflection

Survey 1	Survey 2
• Went from apathetic about math to hating it • Feels unsure about the methods we use • Sounds confused and therefore frustrated that they are unable to be helpful • Despite the parent's worries and frustration, the child likes math • Parent is practicing rote memorization with child: I wonder how I will help them shift their habits? • This parent will need support understanding how to help their child at home	• Went from hating math to apathetic • Admits to lack of confidence and likes technology because it helps them get accurate and correct answers • Despite the parent's worries and lack of confidence in own abilities, the child loves math • I wonder what homework help looks like in this household? • This parent wants communication about the methods and why

This very simple survey gave us quite a bit of information that we can use at the whole-class or individual level. For the whole-class level, notice that both surveys show that the parents want (and need) both examples of the methods that will be used during the school year and the *why* behind those methods. This type of data can help inform us on what to include in unit preview letters or weekly letters at a whole-class level. These data can also help us know how and what to communicate at the parent level. We will explore this idea in the "Parents as Individuals" section in this chapter. Ultimately, communication with parents may not be the same from year to year and might need to be adapted to suit the needs of the current families. Therefore, teachers may need to adjust or adapt their class-level communication from year to year, just like they adapt their instruction of students year to year.

Beginning of the Year Letter From the Teacher

Just like the letter from the school level, a letter from the classroom level is a great way to start off the year with proactive communication. The letters need to be different, as they both play different roles. The whole-school letter sets the expectations for the year and informs parents about the changes in math instruction as a whole. At the classroom level, the letter should focus more on the content taught at that particular grade level and specific ways parents of that age group can support their children. As mentioned previously, if you are in a school that does not have schoolwide communication around expectations in place, then we suggest combining some of Figures 5.1 and 5.2 with Figure 5.6.

> **TIP!**
>
> Attach the beginning of the year letter to the beginning of the year survey if you are sending them by hard copy correspondence. This will potentially indicate the letter was read because the survey was returned. It also limits the number of papers a child has floating around their backpack. If the beginning of the year survey is sent electronically, add a cut-and-sign portion to the beginning of the year letter to hold parents responsible for reading it and to add the two-way communication piece.

Figure 5.6

Beginning of the Year Math Communication

Dear Families,

[Tell parents your goals.]

Welcome to Grade K math! We are excited to work with you and your child to build your child's love of math learning. Our number one goal is to help your child see themselves as a mathematical thinker who sees value in learning math. We also want to help your child see that math is everywhere! To do this, our year-long topics will be taught so that they build on previous understanding and prepare students for future math learning. We will also show students how math is used in the real world.

 [Explain what they can expect their child to learn; keep the educational jargon as simple as possible. Including visuals that match is helpful.]

In Grade K, we will learn lots of math! With your support, your child will learn the following by the end of the school year:

- Count to 100
- Count groups of objects
- Write numbers 0 to 20
- Add and subtract with 5 fluently
- Add and subtract within 10 using objects or drawings
- Use comparison words (e.g., longer, shorter, heavier, lighter)

(Continued)

Intelligent icon source: PeterSnow/iStock.com.

(Continued)

- Identify and describe two- and three-dimensional shapes
- Solve word problems
- And much, much more!

[Explain how they can help their child and feel confident they are doing the right thing.]

Lots of parents ask how they can help their child with math at home. While we take care of teaching the content, there are many ways you can support your child's learning at home.

1. Ask your child questions! Having them explain will often help both them and you understand the math concept being taught.
2. Be curious about the methods, strategies, and approaches we are using. Resist the temptation to show your children the way you learned it. It can create confusion!
3. Talk positively about math and your experiences with math at home. Also, find math in everyday situations (e.g., patterns in floor tiles) and talk about it!
4. Play games! Math is all about problem-solving and games allow children experiences making decisions and choices that often have to do with math.
5. When in doubt, ask us if what you are doing is supporting your child's learning or interfering with it. We are happy to work one-on-one to provide specific guidance!

[List resources for parents to check out. Keep the list between three and five items to prevent resource abundance!]

RECOMMENDED MATH RESOURCES FOR YOUR HOME

Apps

- Bedtime Math, http://bedtimemath.org (available for iPhones, Androids, and computers)

Bedtime Math is striving to help families introduce math as a fun part of their daily routine, as common and beloved as the bedtime story. Within just one school year, kids who did Bedtime Math improved their math achievement on average by 3 months more than children who didn't. Better yet, kids of the most math-anxious parents who chose to do Bedtime Math had gains of half a school year.

Books

- *Adding Parents to the Equation: Understanding Your Child's Elementary School Math* by Dr. Hilary Kreisberg and Dr. Matthew Beyranevand (2019)

This book explains to parents why math instruction is different than in the past, how it's better for our kids, and what you can do at home to support your child's math learning.

- *Everyone Can Learn Math* by Alice Aspinall (2018)

This book is perfect for children to help them build confidence in math. In the book, the main character comes to understand that learning math is no different than learning any other skill in life.

 [List recommended math tools for the home. Keep them grade-level specific and stick to the tools used in your classroom. Name the tool, include a visual, list some areas where the tool is helpful, and list where parents can get the tools if you aren't providing them.]

RECOMMENDED MATH TOOLS FOR YOUR HOME

- **Unifix cubes**—useful for counting, addition, subtraction, and measurement

- **Two-colored counters**—useful for counting, addition, and subtraction

- **Pattern blocks**—useful for identifying and building shapes

- **Rekenreks**—useful for counting, addition, and subtraction

- **Geometric solids**—useful for geometry and identifying three-dimensional shapes

 [Explain how parents can keep up with the math vocabulary.]

Sometimes you may hear your child use a math vocabulary word that is unfamiliar. We will be sending home a Unit Preview Letter before every new unit, where we will list the most important math terms and their definitions. Please use these letters as references throughout the units.

If you have any questions, please reach out!

Warmly,

[Signed Grade K Teachers]

 Available for download at **resources.corwin.com/partneringwithparents/elementary**

Unit Preview Letters

One of the most common asks we have received from parents is a concise overview of each unit before it occurs. Unit preview letters are a great way to inform parents about what math they should expect to see over the next few weeks. This helps them feel familiar with the language they will see and also provides them with examples of some of the math. Many curricular resources already provide letters like this, so be sure to check to see if this already exists. You may want to use a publisher's version as a starting point and personalize it for your class needs. Look at Figure 5.7 to see an example unit preview letter for a third-grade unit on multiplication.

Figure 5.7

Example Unit Preview Letter

Dear Families,

We are excited to start Unit 3 on Multiplication. This is the first time your child will see multiplication. We will build on what they learned in second grade about **repeated addition** to understand making **equal groups** arranged in **arrays**. We will write multiplication equations that represent those arrays.

 [List vocabulary from the unit and define each term.]

In this unit, we will use the following math terms:

- **Array:** the arrangement of objects in rows and columns
- **Commutative Property of Multiplication:** a property of numbers that states we can switch the order of the factors when multiplying and our answers will be the same $(e.g., 3 \times 4 = 4 \times 3)$
- **Distributive Property:** a property of numbers that states we can multiply a number by a group of numbers added together and get the same answer as doing each multiplication separately $(e.g., 4 \times 3 = 4 \times 2 + 4 \times 1)$
- **Equal Groups:** the same number of objects in each set

- **Factor:** a number that gets multiplied

$$2 \times 3 = 6$$
$$\uparrow \quad \uparrow$$

- **Product:** the result of multiplying two or more factors

$$2 \times 3 = 6$$
$$\uparrow$$

- **Repeated Addition:** adding equal groups together

$$2 + 2 + 2 + 2 = 8$$

 [Tell parents what to expect and provide them language.]

You will notice that we will be writing multiplication equations horizontally.

Like This	Not Like This
$4 \times 3 = 12$	$\begin{array}{r} 4 \\ \times 3 \\ \hline 12 \end{array}$

In fourth grade, students will start writing the equations vertically. In third grade, we write equations horizontally so students think flexibly and find multiple strategies to solve them. Please do your best to reinforce writing the equations this way so students focus on understanding before they learn shortcuts and procedures.

We will also be learning three specific strategies to solve multiplication problems. At first students will use colored tiles to build equal groups and arrays, then they will draw those pictures and use numbers, and finally they will write expressions and equations. Below are three different ways students might think about solving 8×7 by the end of the unit.

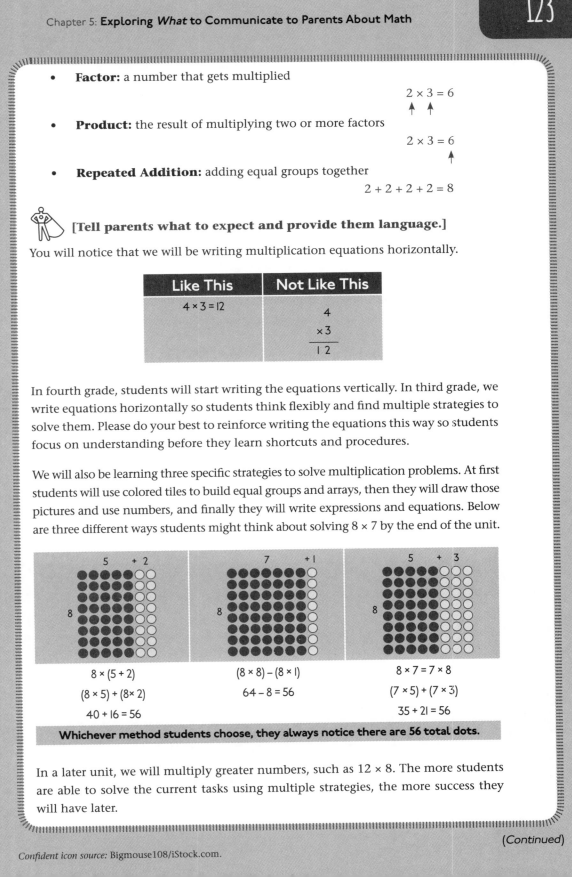

$8 \times (5 + 2)$

$(8 \times 5) + (8 \times 2)$

$40 + 16 = 56$

$(8 \times 8) - (8 \times 1)$

$64 - 8 = 56$

$8 \times 7 = 7 \times 8$

$(7 \times 5) + (7 \times 3)$

$35 + 21 = 56$

Whichever method students choose, they always notice there are 56 total dots.

In a later unit, we will multiply greater numbers, such as 12×8. The more students are able to solve the current tasks using multiple strategies, the more success they will have later.

(Continued)

(Continued)

 [List activities parents can do at home with their kids to support the learning in this particular unit.]

Here are some activities you can try at home:

- Notice multiplication in real-world contexts.
  - o If you are purchasing more than one of the same item at a store, ask your child to round the cost to the nearest dollar and estimate how much you will spend on those items.
  - o Find arrays and ask your child to identify how many objects are in each array by using multiplication (e.g., windows on buildings, floor tiles).
- Build your child's fact fluency using games we learn during this unit.
  - o Play Factor Bingo (students will learn this game and bring home materials to play in Week 2).
  - o Play Multiplication War using a deck of cards (students will learn this game and bring home instructions in Week 1).
- Have your child make their own flashcards.
- Make one side an array and the other side a multiplication equation that matches (e.g., 4 × 5 = 20 would have four rows of five dots).

If you have any questions, please reach out!

Sincerely,

[Signed Teacher or Grade 3 Teachers]

 Available for download at **resources.corwin.com/partneringwithparents/elementary**

Four core wants icon sources: Helpful by appleuzr/iStock.com; Familiar by PeterSnow/iStock.com.

TIP!

Naming and illustrating the strategies you will be teaching in a unit is critical so parents are aware that the number of strategies is finite. In looking back at the parent quotes in Chapter I, you can see that many parents feel there are dozens, if not more, strategies that we teach. Clearly limiting the number of approaches by explicitly stating this in your unit preview letters pushes back on parents' false conception that there are an infinite number of ways to get to an answer, or that the end goal is to be able to solve problems in as many different ways as possible.

Weekly Letters

Weekly letters are a great way to keep parents informed about what their child is learning. Many parents have expressed that they want to know what is happening *before* it happens, so weekly letters are best if they are sent home right before the instruction occurs. These letters do not need to be complex or as detailed as the unit preview letters, but they should show parents what to expect. Figures 5.8 and 5.9 provide examples of weekly letters.

Figure 5.8

Example Weekly Letter, Second Grade

Dear Families,

This week your child will learn to add two numbers between 10 and 99 using a strategy called **partial sums**. Reminder: a **sum** in math is the total, or result, of adding numbers.

When using **partial sums**, break apart each number into smaller parts and then combine all the parts to find the total. This week, we will break apart the numbers by place value (tens and ones). In the future, your child might break apart the numbers differently.

How your child might talk about it:

45 + 56

I can break apart each number by place value: 45 = 40 + 5 and 56 = 50 + 6.

I can add the tens: 40 + 50 = 90

I can add the ones: 5 + 6 = 11

I can add the parts: 90 + 11 = 101

What it might look like mathematically:

$$
\begin{aligned}
45 &= 40 + 5 \\
+\ 56 &= 50 + 6 \\
\hline
101 &= 90 + 11
\end{aligned}
$$

(Continued)

(Continued)

At the end of the week, talk with your child about using **partial sums** to add by asking them to show you how to find the total for 39 + 57 using this strategy. If they struggle, ask these questions:

- Do you think the answer will be greater or less than 100? Why?
- How can you rewrite 39 as tens and ones?
- How can you rewrite 57 as tens and ones?
- What do you get when you add the tens and the tens? The ones and the ones?
- Can you draw your base-ten blocks to help you?

Why we are learning it this way:

Growing up, you may have added numbers like this:

$$\begin{array}{r} \overset{1}{4}5 \\ +56 \\ \hline 101 \end{array}$$

Your child will learn to add numbers like this in fourth grade.

We want to make sure they first understand how our number system works so that when they write it like this, they understand why they are doing the steps.

Look at how the way we are learning connects to the way they will learn it later:

$$\begin{array}{r} 45 = 40 + 5 \\ +56 = 50 + 6 \\ \hline 101 = 90 + 11 \end{array} \qquad \longleftrightarrow \qquad \begin{array}{r} \overset{1}{4}5 \\ +56 \\ \hline 101 \end{array}$$

Students add 5 + 6 and 40 + 50 + 10 in both methods, but writing out the numbers by their place values helps students understand *how much the numbers are worth.* This will help prevent mistakes later on when they get to fourth grade and learn a shorter method.

If you have any questions, please reach out!

Sincerely,

[Signed Teacher or Grade 2 Teachers]

Figure 5.9

Example Weekly Letter, First Grade

Dear Families,

This week your child will learn to add two numbers that result in 11 to 19 using a strategy called **make a ten**. Your child will learn this using a tool called a **ten-frame**.

This is a **ten-frame**. It has ten boxes formed by two rows of five. We use this tool to help students see groups of objects. This helps move them away from counting by ones.

When using **ten-frames**, your child will learn to draw a circle inside each box to represent the numbers being added (called **addends**). For example, 9 + 7 might be represented on the ten-frame like this:

 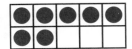

$$9 + 7$$

When using **make a ten**, the goal is for one **addend** to become 10. To do this, we have to take some circles from one ten-frame and move them to the other. This week, we will focus on taking circles from the ten-frame on the right. Next week, we will take from the ten-frame on the left.

How your child might talk about it:

9 + 7

I can take 1 circle from the ten-frame with 7 and move it to the ten-frame with 9.

I now have 10 circles in one ten-frame and 6 circles in the other.

9 + 7 = 10 + 6

I can add the parts: 10 + 6 = 16

(Continued)

(Continued)

What it might look like mathematically:

9 + 7

9 + (1 + 6)

(9 + 1) + 6

10 + 6 = 16

9 + 7 = 10 + 6

At the end of the week, talk with your child about using **making a ten** to add by asking them to show you how to find the total for 8 + 6 using this strategy. If they struggle, ask these questions:

- Do you think the answer will be greater or less than 10? Why?

- What added to 8 gives you 10?

- Can you draw your ten-frames and circles to help you?

Why we are learning it this way:

Growing up, you may have learned to add 9 + 7 by simply memorizing the fact. Memorizing can be challenging for students and does not help them when they move on to more challenging math. By using the make a ten strategy for addition, students deepen their understanding of our place value system and the relationships between numbers. They will continue to use this strategy throughout their schooling by adjusting to make a multiple of ten when they are adding greater numbers at the end of first grade and throughout second grade and also adjusting to make a whole with measurement in third grade and fractions in fourth grade.

If you have any questions, please reach out!

Sincerely,

[Signed Teacher or Grade 1 Teachers]

 Available for download at **resources.corwin.com/partneringwithparents/elementary**

TIP!

If you do not plan on sending home both unit preview letters *and* weekly letters, then consider how you could combine the two so parents get as much information as possible in their one correspondence.

These weekly letters offer specific guidance that addresses parents' four core wants. Parents are informed about the strategies and methods so they feel intelligent and knowledgeable, they are given resources to support at home so they feel helpful, they are shown why the math is being taught the way it is so they feel confident, and they are provided vocabulary terms and definitions so they feel familiar with the language. To enhance the two-way communication, consider adding to your weekly letter a task for parents and a signature line to show you they did the task. You can make it a cut-and-sign form so the bottom portion comes back to you, or you can use the agenda notebook insert format as previously referenced in Chapter 4 (Figure 4.8). If you use an Edtech app, you can also consider posting Figure 5.10 in the app.

Figure 5.10

Reflection of Weekly Letter

Dear Families,

Please check one and sign below by Monday.

- ❏ I asked my child and they taught me the strategy successfully.
- ❏ I asked my child and they needed me to ask some of the questions provided, but they eventually got it.
- ❏ I asked my child, but they struggled. Please let me know what else I can do to help.
- ❏ I did not ask, but will soon.

Signature

X _____

online resources ↖   Available for download at **resources.corwin.com/partneringwithparents/elementary**

TIP!

For more success, reprint the "why are we learning it this way" portion of Figure 5.8 and all of Figure 5.9 onto one small copy and staple it to the Saturday/Sunday calendar page in the child's agenda notebook if sent by hard copy. This will prevent the papers from getting lost. For an example, look back at Figure 4.8 in Chapter 4.

This acts as a mini-progress update for parents because they get to see first-hand whether or not their child can do the assigned task, and it provides you a bit more information on which children you might provide some intervention.

Mid- and End-of-Year Surveys From the Teacher

As educators, we use and hear the terms *formative and summative assessment* ad nauseum, but generally we use them in the context of our students. We believe that assessing our own practices through the lens of parents is a critical component to improving our practice. At the whole-class level, consider sending one or two surveys to get feedback from parents. A mid-year survey is meant for gathering formative data and the results will inform you on how best to adjust your efforts in order to make your communication more meaningful and useful for parents (Figure 5.11). An end-of-year survey is more summative and will give you feedback on your year as a whole, but it can also act formatively by giving feedback that might help you adjust your practice the following school year (Figure 5.12).

Figure 5.11

Example Mid-Year Survey

1. Before each math unit starts, I send home Unit Preview Letters that show you what your child will be learning, explain the vocabulary used in the unit, show you the strategies we will be learning, and offer resources for supporting your child at home. How helpful have those been for you?
   - ❏ Very helpful
   - ❏ Somewhat helpful
   - ❏ Not helpful at all

2. What are some ways I can improve my communication about math?
   - ❏ More personalized communication about my child's progress
   - ❏ More information about why math looks different than when I was a child

❏ Offer a beginning of unit optional parent webinar where you teach me the math

❏ I think your communication is just enough! I don't need more.

❏ Other: _____

3. Which communication types do you find helpful? (Check all that apply.)

❏ Beginning of the year overview

❏ Unit preview letters before each unit is taught

❏ Weekly letters before each week's content is taught

❏ Information on supporting your child in math

❏ Other: _____

4. How satisfied are you with my communication about math?

❏ Very satisfied

❏ Satisfied

❏ Unsatisfied

If you answered unsatisfied, please explain: _____

_____

_____

5. How satisfied are you with the frequency of my communication (how often it happens)?

❏ Very satisfied

❏ Satisfied

❏ Unsatisfied

If you answered unsatisfied, please explain: _____

_____

_____

Your answers to this survey will help me improve my communication about math for the rest of the year. What else do you think is important that I know?

_____

_____

Figure 5.12

Example End-of-Year Survey Questions

This year, you received a beginning of the year overview of what your child will be learning in math, letters before each unit was taught showing you the math your child will learn, and weekly letters about what to expect each week and how to help at home. Please reflect on the year to answer these survey questions.

1. What about my communication about math this year did you find most helpful? (Check one.)
   - ❏ Beginning of the year overview
   - ❏ Unit preview letters before each unit is taught
   - ❏ Weekly letters before each week's content is taught
   - ❏ Information on supporting your child in math
   - ❏ It was all helpful
   - ❏ Other: _____

2. What about my communication about math this year did you find least helpful? (Check one.)
   - ❏ Beginning of the year overview
   - ❏ Unit preview letters before each unit is taught
   - ❏ Weekly letters before each week's content is taught
   - ❏ Information on supporting your child in math
   - ❏ It was all helpful
   - ❏ Other: _____

3. Which communication types do you hope your child's teacher next year uses to communicate about math? (Check all that apply.)
   - ❏ Beginning of the year overview
   - ❏ Unit preview letters before each unit is taught
   - ❏ Weekly letters before each week's content is taught
   - ❏ Information on supporting your child in math
   - ❏ Other: _____

 Available for download at **resources.corwin.com/partneringwithparents/elementary**

TIP!

Add an optional "comment" section after each closed-ended question. We have found in our surveys of parents that many use the comment box to qualify their choices and it provides more information for you.

The surveys can be short and simple and should focus on what you are most interested in learning about. Another aspect we love about these surveys is they can act as documentation for your practice. Many states evaluate teachers on their communication and family engagement. The surveys and results can be used as evidence toward these standards. Administrators can work at a schoolwide level to co-develop the surveys and ensure they are offered at the classroom level.

Whether you send one survey or two, be sure to use questions that give you information on what you are truly interested in learning more about.

REACHING PARENTS AS INDIVIDUALS

Individual communication with parents plays a vastly different role than the other two types of communication. The focus of individual communication is less about general information or the math their child will be learning and is more dedicated to specifics about their child's progress. In a school with ongoing, high-quality math communication at the school and classroom levels, parents may need individual communication less frequently because many of their questions will be answered proactively; they might feel so well informed that they don't need to follow up individually.

Think back to the survey we presented in the Chapter 1 Apply It! exercise and revisited with real parent responses in Figure 5.4. Using the data from the beginning of the year survey can help inform your individual communication and can serve as a great initial conversation starter. For example, look at one parent's response to the following question:

> **Question:** What else do you think I should know that will help me understand how to support you and your child's math learning this year?
>
> **Parent Response:** Is it acceptable to show your work and get the right answer if it is not the method that is being taught at the moment?

You could flag this response and respond to this question in your first individual communication with this parent (in whatever capacity, such as phone, email, etc.). This helps the parent see that communication is two way and that you read what they say. This parent asked a great question; while only one parent wrote it, others might be thinking it. In addition to the specific individual-level follow-up, you could also respond in a whole-class manner through an FAQ posted to the website or embedded in the first unit preview letter.

Individual communication also involves communicating about a child's progress. As mentioned previously, speaking from a strengths-based perspective is critical for this type of communication. Consider initiating this communication between the second to fourth week of school to introduce yourself and share some positive information about the child's math learning. This will model how to praise effort, perseverance, process, and high expectations for the parent, which is what you hope they will do for their child. In addition, using the results from the beginning of the year survey can help guide your initial conversation. For example, look at a different parent's responses to the same survey:

> **Question:** The following best describes your attitude toward math when you were a child.
>
> **Answer:** Hated it. I wasn't taught properly. When I asked a question all I got back was, "Well if you listened." I was. It was hard for me even when I asked for help.
>
> **Question:** What else do you think I should know that will help me understand how to support you and your child's math learning this year?
>
> **Answer:** Don't ever tell them they weren't listening. They could be trying to keep up. Encourage asking questions. So kids don't feel embarrassed about the help they need.

So much can be learned from this parent's responses. This parent obviously did not feel seen, heard, respected, or safe in math class and wants their child to experience the opposite. Imagine the feeling of trust, respect, and support this parent will have if you greet them with an initial positive communication that specifically addresses their concerns; for example, highlight that one of your classroom norms is to help students feel safe and ask questions, and state that you won't repeat this parent's experience with their child. Just picture if this parent received a note or phone call that said this:

> *I read your survey response and felt the pain you experienced growing up in math class. I promise not to repeat that experience with your child. One of our classroom norms is to ask questions until ideas make sense. In this class, we value processing time and questioning for understanding. I want your child to feel safe to ask questions and learn. Please let me know if your child ever experiences otherwise.*

This one individual interaction could prevent a host of future issues.

When it comes to one-on-one communication, it is also important to be specific. A parent of a third grader and a sixth grader shared her frustrations with general feedback. She said,

> *Instead of saying kids need to know facts . . . give me something targeted. For example, tell me my kid needs to work on their 6 and 7 facts. Be specific. When people are told to do everything, they shut down.*

Contrast the specificity of offering resources to a parent for helping their child improve their 6 and 7 facts to simply and generally asking a parent to support their child's multiplication facts. There are 144 basic multiplication facts we expect children to know or be able to access fluently. Reducing this load—to say, 14 facts (6×6 through 6×12 and 7×6 through 7×12)—helps target the parents' help, makes it easier for them to know where to start, and avoids having them spend time on facts their child may actually have mastered.

Other factors to consider during individual communication are the work and mathematical habits of the child. What strategies have you observed during daily work that bring the child success? You may notice that some students benefit greatly when they work collaboratively with a peer prior to attempting to solve a problem independently. Other students may perform better by working silently at their own pace with access to an anchor chart or reference from the lesson. Some students may need to sketch out or doodle ideas until they develop an understanding of the concept. Each student has their own way of learning mathematics; as a teacher, you get the front-row seat to observing these behaviors in action! Individual communication can include these findings so parents can encourage their children to access these same strategies when they are working at home.

After you have had your initial positive correspondence, individual communication with parents will vary according to their wants and student needs. Be sure to make all communication from a strengths-based perspective, include how you are supporting the child during school time with math, and offer useful resources for parents to try at home to help students improve in specific areas.

PUTTING IT ALL TOGETHER

In this chapter, we explored what makes communication with parents effective, reflected on ways to communicate proactively about math, and thought critically about how to use the data from two-way communication to improve the delivery of information to parents. Parent events are additional ways to provide communication. We will explore various types of parent events in Chapter 6.

FREQUENTLY ASKED QUESTIONS

Q **I love the idea of beginning of the year surveys and letters, unit preview letters, and all of the communication ideas you have written about, but it seems like it would take a lot of time that I just don't have. What suggestions do you have for teachers who don't have time to make them?**

A You are absolutely right; this does take time to craft thoughtfully. However, the time is certainly worth the investment. The more proactive teachers and school leaders are in communicating, the less parental involvement becomes an issue and the more parents can help educators accomplish their math learning goals for all students. Our first suggestion is to check with your curricular resource to see if they already have family letters and supports that you could use instead of starting from scratch. We also encourage you to work with your grade-level team and school leaders to see about structures that can be put in place to support the development of this work, such as common planning time. Depending on the number of grade-level teachers on your team, you could also divide and conquer your efforts, each taking on the task of making one or some of the stated items.

Q **Believe it or not, I have tried most of these communication methods but there are still some parents who are unresponsive and their children are the ones struggling. Help please!**

A Good for you for not giving up. Parent communication, especially around mathematics, is challenging. Because we don't know all the factors (such as home life), it is best to assume positive intent. Continue to reach out to the parent in a variety of ways. One method may prove better than another. Some parents find in-person meetings are the best way for them to receive communication. In-person meetings could serve as an opportunity to assist them in seeing the value and the "how-to" of the preferred mode of communication.

Q **I am an elementary teacher who teaches all subjects. I understand the importance of this communication about math, but I also have to communicate about three other subjects. Is it really important to pull out the math communication as suggested or can I combine it how I see fit within other subject communication?**

A This is a great question and one that is best answered by you! Knowing what your parents need, much like knowing your students' needs, will guide that decision. Many parents are heavily concerned with mathematics. For this reason, sending separate communication about mathematics might prove helpful for putting parents at ease. You certainly can embed the communication in conjunction with other subjects, but we suggest finding ways to highlight the mathematics if that is an identified need of your parents.

APPLY IT! TEACHER ACTIVITIES

How Will You Improve *What* You Communicate?

1. Take a look back at all the suggestions we provided in this chapter. What is one strategy you have yet to try? Take some time and try it out.

2. Consider the importance of communicating with parents as a class and parents as individuals.

   a. Which type of communication do you do more often?

   b. What makes the two types of communication different?

   c. How can you improve both areas?

APPLY IT! SCHOOL LEADER ACTIVITIES

How Will You Improve *What* You Communicate?

1. Take a look back at all the suggestions we provided in this chapter. Which of them do you find most important for your teachers to do? Choose one that you want to ensure all teachers are implementing. Develop an action plan to help the teachers put the work in place. Consider the following:

   a. What structures need to be in place for this to work?

   b. What barriers to success might exist?

   c. What resources can you provide your staff to make this happen?

2. Take a moment to think about your own parent communication. How could you improve your work and model for your staff what you expect them to do?

CHAPTER 6

Hosting Parent Events

What is the most underused resource in education today?
This resource can increase student engagement and
achievement and decrease a teacher's workload.
The answer? Parents.

— Lauren Tripp Barlis

Generally, we remember a small amount of what we read, a little more of what we see, even more of what we discuss with others, and an even greater amount of what we personally experience. If we truly want parents to see themselves as partners in and supporters of their child's mathematical learning, then we need to find ways to have them *experience* the mathematics their children are learning today. In this chapter, we explore a variety of ideas for how schools can empower parents through meaningful learning experiences.

IN THIS CHAPTER YOU WILL . . .

- Read real examples of successes and challenges from school leaders and teachers with regard to hosting parent events,
- Explore a variety of ways to involve parents in experiencing and learning about 21st century mathematics teaching and learning, and
- Consider the aspect of accessibility in all events you may plan.

Icon source: Enis Aksoy/iStock.com.

PARENT EXPERIENCES

As we've discussed, many parents have limited exposure to seeing the way math is taught today; they simply haven't had first-hand experience to understand the worth. We believe one of the best ways to help parents see the value of the way we teach math today is to host experiential learning opportunities.

There are many different events schools can host that provide parents a variety of learning experiences. Some events are nonspecific to mathematics, whereas others are math specific. Here are some examples:

Events Nonspecific to Math

- Back to School Nights
- Parent–Teacher Conferences

Math-Specific Events

- Family Math Nights
- Parent Math Nights
- Family Math Days and Math Mornings
- Parent Book Clubs
- Mystery Mathematicians

We have found that parents yearn for math-specific information at events that are nonspecific to mathematics, or they want to be offered more math-specific events and access to the information gleaned if they cannot physically attend. No matter which events your school chooses to offer, be sure they provide parents enough math-specific support to satiate their four core wants—making them feel helpful, intelligent, confident, and familiar.

We hope you can walk away from this chapter with some fresh new ideas to try. But we also recognize that we do not know your specific context and that some of these ideas may just not be feasible, or they might require major "renovations" to make them work for you and your school's population. There is no "right" way to host these events. In fact, in all the interviews we conducted, we did not hear the same thing twice. Each and every school or district offers unique versions of these events that meet the direct needs of the parents and community. This means that not all of the ideas we share will be applicable for your school or setting, so it is up to you to determine what works best or consider tailoring ideas to meet your community's needs.

EVENTS NONSPECIFIC TO MATH

Some events, often schoolwide, include math but are not specific to math. Given that these events tend to be highly attended, it is important to take advantage of the opportunity to offer families quick mathematics guidance and support. Two commonly held nonspecific to math events are Back to School Nights and parent–teacher conferences.

Back to School Nights

If there is one consistent event that happens at most schools, it is curriculum nights or open houses, more commonly known as Back to School Nights. These events tend to be the most attended event of the school year. They happen early in the beginning of the year, parents are eager to meet the teacher, and they present an opportunity for parents to hear about the year to come. Generally, this event offers very little content-specific time and even less one-on-one time with individual parents. Even with a minimal amount of time dedicated to mathematics, this is the perfect opportunity to sneak in some information about why math looks different today than it did in the past.

Ways to Communicate About Mathematics During Back to School Night

- Include in your presentation a slide or two with an overview of the year's mathematics content, a brief explanation about why we teach mathematics differently, and some general ways parents can support their children at home.
- Use transition times intentionally. As parents enter the classroom, have a sense-making routine warm-up ready to go that you would normally do with students. This will give parents a glimpse of what teaching mathematics for understanding looks like.
- Provide handouts about mathematics this year. This is a great time to give parents your beginning of the year letter, flyers about upcoming math-specific events they can attend, and guidance for how to support their child at home.

(Continued)

(Continued)

- Before Back to School Night, have your students create a sense-making math task for their parent to solve. As parents enter the classroom, each desk will have a puzzle or sense-making task that their child has made for them with love.
- Before Back to School Night, take short video footage of your class engaged in an authentic mathematics task or a sense-making routine. During Back to School Night, share a glimpse into what math class looks like today.
- Be sure your room is filled with anchor charts or posters made by students highlighting important mathematics you want the parents to know about, such as classroom or schoolwide norms (e.g., mistakes are learning opportunities), pictures of student work showing a variety of methods to solve a task, careers that use mathematics, mathematical autobiographies, or mathematical habits we want students to elicit.

 To find example handouts to provide families at Back-to-School Night, visit **resources.corwin.com/ partneringwithparents**

Parent–Teacher Conferences

Parent–teacher conferences are a popular school initiative that offers parents an opportunity to meet the teacher individually and hear about their child's progress and performance. We contend that if teachers and school leaders are engaged in ongoing communication throughout the year, these conferences would then be less centered around updating and more about collaboratively working together to determine how to support the child in reaching their goals.

Parent–teacher conferences review the child's efforts as a whole child—academically, socially, and emotionally. They also tend to be short, sometimes even as short as 15 minutes, and often don't occur until several months into the school year. These types of conferences should not serve as a place for new information, but rather as a quick check-in and an opportunity for face-to-face connection. Making use of the ways we suggest communicating in Chapters 4 and 5 will allow these conferences to be more about the child's work. To elevate these conferences, we suggest hosting student–parent–teacher conferences, or three-way conferences. Doing so allows the child to lead the session, helps the student take ownership, and keeps the adults focused on the child.

Like the other structures we discussed in Chapter 3, it is important that all stakeholders are aware of their role, especially as it pertains to mathematics, during the conference. Consider providing a handout for parents and students outlining their responsibilities during the conference, specific to mathematics (Figure 6.1).

Figure 6.1 – Three-Way Mathematics Conference Roles

Student, Parent, and Teacher Roles With Conferences		
Student	Parent	Teacher
• Reflects on their mathematics performance and effort, focusing on strengths • Shares work samples and why they chose them • Tells about self-identified areas of improvement • Describes goals they will set for themselves	• Praises the student's effort and identifies strengths in the student's work • Asks questions about the shared work samples or content to better understand the mathematics • Describes goals they want to see from the student if not mentioned • Identifies ways to help the student reach their goals from the home front	• Praises the student's effort and identifies strengths in the student's work • Updates the parent and child as to next content topics and expectations • Describes goals they want to see from the student if not mentioned

online resources ⟋ Available for download at **resources.corwin.com/partneringwithparents/elementary**

Also consider using class time to have students reflect on their work, choose work samples to share, and prepare for the conference. This helps teach students other important skills, such as time management, justifying their thinking, and critical thinking. Create a guided template for students to use to help them prepare. Include reflection questions such as these:

- How were you a mathematician this term?
- What could you improve mathematically?
- What challenged you mathematically this term?
- What was your proudest moment in math this term?
- What do you want your family to notice when they look at your math work?
- What are your goals for next term in math?

For students in kindergarten and first grade, consider providing sentence starters instead of questions and include large, empty boxes so students can draw their reflections.

If you do not host three-way conferences, we still highly recommend that you clarify the roles before the start of the conference and take on the student role by identifying important math work samples that will highlight newer math strategies or vocabulary that parents could learn.

MATH-SPECIFIC EVENTS

Some events are specific to math. Hosting math-specific events truly depends on the community needs and school structures. So rather than offer a "how-to," we will share what others have done and provide support templates in the online resources to help you get started.

We want to recognize the school leaders and educators who took time to share with us their experiences in running math-specific events. We have learned a lot from them and hope you will, too.

Family Math Nights

Family Math Nights are events used to engage whole families, not just parents, in playing, building, and puzzling and help families understand the math their children are learning and ways to incorporate math at home.

As Dan Finkel famously stated in his 2016 TEDx Talk, "What books are to reading, play is to mathematics." **Family Math Nights** are events used to engage whole families, not just parents, in this exact idea—that playing, building, and puzzling are ways we can help our children develop mathematical thinking habits that apply well beyond traditional school mathematics. Family Math Nights, when designed well, offer parents opportunities to:

- **See** how math is taught today and why it is taught the way it is,
- **Engage** in play and conversations with their child that can be replicated at home, and
- **Observe** the art of questioning children's thinking to focus on mathematical habits and processes.

Four core wants icon sources: Helpful by appleuzr/iStock.com; Intelligent by PeterSnow/iStock.com; Confident by Bigmouse108/iStock.com; Familiar by PeterSnow/iStock.com.

Family Math Nights can be organized in a variety of different ways and don't always have to be offered at night. There is no right or wrong way to make it your own, but it is important to remember that this is a big event, often schoolwide—many of the folks we interviewed compared it to planning a wedding. It takes time, patience, dedication, and organization to truly make the event a success. In this section, we share poignant vignettes from others who have hosted Family Math Nights and offer a variety of options that may support you.

Dr. Molly Rawding, a math coach in Massachusetts, has been hosting parent math events for the past 5 years. In 2019, she hosted a Family Math Night where the attendance outdid any of her past events: it drew 225 attendees! After 4 years of trying out different structures for the event and adjusting based on feedback, she was impressively satisfied with the result. Her secret? She found what worked for her population of parents. For them, it was organizing an event that centered on a theme—in this case, she created a Family Math Night centered around puzzling. She even titled the event accordingly, "Perfectly Puzzled." It was also all about involving the children. She recognized over the years that the more children were involved, the more her attendance increased.

To make the event what it is, Molly reminds us how collaborating with teachers and other school leaders is critical during the planning phases, especially when determining what is important to share with parents. Using her experience, parent feedback from past events, collaboration with another math specialist, and her colleagues' suggestions based on their everyday parent communication, Molly and her team of teachers collectively decided to focus on puzzling to target the idea of supporting productive struggle at home. Molly shared,

> One of the big takeaways we wanted to share with parents was how important it is for their children to see them persevere, or puzzle through something. It was important that we chose good tasks and interesting puzzles, and that we provided a structure where working together was clearly defined as asking questions, not rushing to an answer, and collaborating—modeling for parents that it is okay that they don't know everything right from the get-go.

To do this, she structured her 90-minute Family Math Night by starting with a 15-minute overview, where she and several volunteer teachers framed the session by describing the goals and agenda, showed a short video about the research behind 21st century mathematics teaching

TIP!

Once your school gets to a place where parents understand the shifts in math education and no longer need an overview of why math instruction looks different today than it did in the past, your introduction at Family Math Nights can focus on other topics, such as habits of mathematical thinkers, ways to engage children in mathematical thinking at home, and more.

and learning, discussed the importance of coming together for a night like this, and shared one to two personal anecdotes about math, often focused on speed, memorization, or some negative experience they have had. Molly finds that this story segment creates a space for parents to relate and helps them realize that even teachers may not have had good experiences learning math growing up, but that they, too, want better for the children.

The teachers then gave everyone a challenging estimation task to ensure parents were actively engaged in productive struggle (the theme). The parents turned and talked with their children, learning about a strategy used in school to communicate. After 5–10 minutes of parent–child think-pair-shares, the teachers brought the whole group back together and engaged the audience to share some ideas. The teachers then helped bridge the connection for how a task such as the one they explored together could be done at home. This process continued for 60 more minutes; every 20 minutes the families were assigned a different puzzle or task and asked to engage in it as learners. All the while, the teachers walked around to assist as needed, modeled how to question someone's process instead of answering or "rescuing" them, and looked for critical thinking moves or math behaviors that they could highlight as a whole group after each task. The entire event took place in the school's gymnasium, where families sat together at tables and experienced what it is like to learn in today's classroom and saw first-hand how the role of a teacher has shifted over the years.

In thinking about Molly's story, what stands out the most for us is that her success came after years of perseverance. She found what worked for her and her community by testing ideas and, most importantly, surveying for feedback. She used the feedback to improve her construction of the event.

Aly Martinez is a mathematics instructional coordinator and former high school math educator in California. Much like Molly, Aly has also found that using puzzles and games as the "main event" has helped in her Family Math Night endeavors. Her story is a bit different, however, in that she saw a need within her own community, as *a parent*, and acted on it. Wanting to give back to her community but, more importantly, provide her son an experience she felt he deserved, Aly did everything she could to support her son's school in hosting its first Family Math Night—all the way down to actually taking on the entire endeavor herself. After offering one successful Family Math Night for her son's school, she then continued offering these events at other local schools in the district.

Aly has one main goal for her Family Math Nights, or Family Game Nights as she calls them, and that is that folks leave knowing how to become a math family, an idea she got from the University of Chicago. The University of Chicago's "Becoming a Math Family" website shares three guiding principles:

1. Math is a process,
2. Math is everywhere, and
3. Math is social.

Using the three guiding principles as her theoretical framework, Aly ensures that by the end of the night, parents know these three beliefs by heart. In fact, each event starts with the reading aloud of a Commitment Pledge that parents vow to follow throughout the night and then they repeat the pledge again at the end of the night as a commitment moving forward. Look at Figure 6.2 to see Aly's Parent Commitment Pledge.

> **TIP!**
>
> Are you interested in learning more about **becoming a math family** or using some of these resources for your Family Math Nights? Learn more here: https://becomingamathfamily.uchicago.edu/.

Figure 6.2 – Aly Martinez's Parent Commitment Pledge

Parent Commitment Pledge

We commit to becoming math families by:

- Playing games at home
- Asking questions to learn about the *process*
- *Talking about* numbers, patterns, and thinking at home
- Looking for math in *our everyday lives*

Aly wants her Family Game Nights to be fun, so each event starts with a 30-minute community math time where she lines the auditorium with long, rectangular tables and fills the room with math manipulatives, puzzles, and play. During this community math time, families engage in logic puzzles, estimation jars, symmetry games, and much, much more—all connected by their underlying theme: math. Her intent is to create a mingling space for the community with conversations focused on math, connection, and play.

Once families have had a chance to mingle, network, and engage in play, they join Aly as a whole group and she conducts a short Three-Act Math Task. A **Three-Act Math Task**, created by Dan Meyer (2011), is a math task presented as a story with three parts: Act 1, Provocation

Three-Act Math Task: A math task presented as a story with three parts: Act I, Provocation (the hook); Act 2, Information (the climax); and Act 3, Check of Solution (the reveal).

(the hook); Act 2, Information (the climax); and Act 3, Check of Solution (the reveal). Her intent in modeling a Three-Act Math Task is to help families see how the elements of questioning and talking about numbers and patterns are incorporated in the way math is taught today and to engage them in all the things she is asking them to commit to in their pledge. She also wants them to see the three guiding principles in action. The Three-Act Math Task is not about speed or accuracy; rather, it is about the process and is very social in its structure.

Following Aly's whole-group math task where she models for parents what math class today looks and feels like, students and their families run off with a treasure map on a mission to complete a puzzle or task in each room. Each room has a teacher and a high school student volunteer there for support and guidance. Parents and students can choose to go to whichever room they want in any order they'd like. They earn a stamp on their treasure map for each room completed, and the map is collected at the end of the night for a chance to win the big raffle prize. Aly strategically prints her feedback forms on the back of the treasure map that kids hold onto like a prized possession, knowing they could win the raffle. This ensures she gets a good amount of feedback that she can use moving forward.

It is important to note that Aly takes her data collection seriously. She has a spreadsheet for each event, where she tallies the number of attendees and inputs all the participant responses from the feedback forms so she can review them holistically and determine how to improve each event. One of the questions on the feedback form asks, "What did you learn about math education by participating in this event?" Among the hundreds of responses showing that families valued the time together and learned that math can be social and fun, one response in particular stood out to us. It said in Spanish, "Que la matemáticas son divertidos en familia," which translates to "That math is fun as a family."

Another parent said, "that you can do math with anything you have at home." These two parents (and the hundreds of others who said similar things) have grasped the greatest advice that a Family Math Night could offer: that math is something everyone can do, anywhere. Even with all the informative responses, Aly still reflects that she is continuously working to improve the questions. She said,

> I always get some responses where someone writes what they think
> I want to hear—like "I learned how to count" or "I learned how to

subtract"—and I can tell when those responses show up that I need to work on the question because it's not giving me everything that I want and need to know.

As we have shown in previous chapters, surveying for feedback is only useful when the survey gives you information that is helpful.

Aly's feedback form also includes a question that asks parents to reflect on what made the event successful. Of the choices, "materials to take home," "learning about games," "timing," and "event theme" were most popular across all the Family Game Nights she's hosted. This information is important; it tells Aly that her theme of "games" helped parents decide to attend and that providing parents with all the materials helped them see the value of the night because now they can continue to play with math at home.

Aly shared that her initial Family Game Night planning was based on what she appreciated most as a parent, such as movement, interactivity, food, the ability to take the materials home, and so on. She adjusted from there based on parent responses from the feedback forms. To do this was no easy feat. Aly raised over $7,000 through grant funding and donations. She says that physically going to local businesses and sharing about ways they can support the local Family Game Night is how she has been most successful. She uses these community partnerships, with local car dealers, casinos, museums, restaurants, and others, to obtain donations of food, guest passes for the raffle, decks of cards for the games, and more.

Reflecting on Aly's story, it is clear that Aly is passionate about ensuring that her Family Game Nights are just what the community needs. While she has an educator background, the real driver here is the fact that she is an actual community member, one who wants to offer her time and talent to bring people together around a topic she holds near and dear to her heart. Many teachers and school leaders reading Aly's story may be thinking, "I don't have time to run to local businesses and do the hustle Aly did!" Yet we hope you take away from Aly's story that community matters. Consider finding a parent in your community who, like Aly, wants to give back. They are there. You just have to find them.

Molly and Aly's Family Math Nights, while different in structure and format, also share many overlaps, especially when it comes to building capacity. In both cases, it is clear that the success came from perseverance and using data to inform and adjust future events. For Molly, engaging six to seven teachers is both a form of support and

TIP!

When you create a feedback form for a Family Math Night, decide what is important to know from the families. Are you trying to identify whether the timing or day of the event was well chosen? Are you eager to know what the parents learned? Are you looking to understand if the presenters were effective? Ultimately, choose questions that both help you plan a more successful future event and provide you evidence of success. Most importantly, try to keep the feedback form brief (four to five questions maximum), as you will likely have parents fill out the form before they head home.

also a way to empower educators. They do the math together ahead of the evening and even do a dress rehearsal the night before to ensure everyone is ready. Aly has used her high school educator background to develop a group called "Future Teachers" at the local high school. High schoolers who want to become teachers join and run some of the Family Math Night stations alongside actual educators, gaining wonderful experience that they otherwise would not receive and also providing Aly the much needed support. As teachers and school leaders know, Family Math Nights can support more than just parents.

Looking for sample Family Math Night schedules? Here is a summary of Molly and Aly's Family Math Nights.

Family Math Night Possible Schedules

Molly's Family Math Night	Aly's Family Game Night
6:00–6:20 Introductions	4:30–5:00 Community Math Happy Hour
6:20–6:40 Math Task 1 and Debrief	5:00–5:15 Welcome and Math Task
6:40–7:00 Math Task 2 and Debrief	5:15–5:30 Rotation 1
7:00–7:20 Math Task 3 and Debrief	5:30–5:45 Rotation 2
7:20–7:30 Closure and Call to Action	5:45–6:00 Rotation 3
	6:00–6:10 Raffles and Prizes

The through line across all the Family Math Night stories shared is that the event is not as much about the content itself and helping parents understand the *how*, but more about creating an experience that helps parents realize that math is fun, recognize how they can support at home in more playful ways, and understand that math is something that everyone can do. However, this can be challenging to achieve if parents do not attend.

Trish Kepler is the director of Nursery-5 Mathematics in Connecticut. She has realized that one of the best ways to address the families who do not attend is to develop a website devoted to curating all the resources from parent math events. She said,

> *Parents are busy, families are busy, the evenings are hard. And as much as we try to schedule at different times to capture different audiences, it's impossible to bring in everyone. . . . so we want to make sure that even if they can't take advantage of the face-to-face opportunities, we are still sharing the learning that was taking place at the event with them.*

Chad Williams, a third-grade teacher in Canada, suggests adding QR codes or links to short webinars or videos that explain the handouts or resources for parents who cannot attend the live events. Since misinformation spreads easily, Chad worries that handouts without a corresponding video or explanation are left to the parents' interpretation. He has found in his work that providing an extra video resource gives parents the added confidence to engage in dialogue with their child.

> **TIP!**
> Consider recording your parent event so you can offer the experience to parents who could not attend.

No matter what, parents who do not attend the live event will not receive the same experience. Ultimately, it is critical that if our end goal is to reach *all* parents, just like we want to reach *all* learners when we teach, then we must put structures in place to support those who cannot physically attend the events. This might mean creating a webpage, like Trish, or recording parts of the event and spending a few extra hours making a short video that parents can watch from the comfort of their home, like Chad. It also might mean offering the event in a hybrid manner, where some people attend live and others attend virtually if your school is capable technology-wise. Or you might choose to offer a fully remote experience for parents, in which you provide the link and families can log on, learn a game, and then be placed in breakout rooms to play the game with other families at similar grade levels. However you decide to increase your accessibility, be sure to continue to strive for improvement, using intentionally designed questionnaires and feedback forms to drive your adjustments.

- Host a Family *Learning* Night instead of Family *Math* Night and incorporate more than just math. Many parents struggle to make it to school for even one event, so combine many events into one.
- Consider how you name the event. The more fun it sounds, the more likely your attendance will increase.
- Reach out to local businesses and create community partnerships for donations and funding for your event.

 To download sample resources to support your Family Math Night, visit **resources.corwin.com/ partneringwithparents/elementary**

Parent Math Nights

Have you ever heard the quote, "Information is the currency of democracy" (n.d.)? The more informed people are, the better decisions they can make. This is exactly why Parent Math Nights exist. **Parent Math Nights** are events meant to inform parents about the math we teach today so that they are equipped with accurate

> **Parent Math Nights** are events meant to inform parents about the math we teach today so that they are equipped with accurate information.

information. Parent Math Nights, when designed well, offer parents opportunities to:

- **Learn** about strategies, models, and tools that are commonly used today and why math instruction has changed over time, and
- **Experience** the math their child is learning so they can better support at home.

Although Parent Math Nights (or Parent University, as some districts call similar events) may offer childcare or have children engaging in math activities in a separate space, this event differs from Family Math Nights in that the focus is often more content heavy and parents are not learning alongside and from their children. Like we stated at the beginning of the chapter, you can make any event your own and do what you want with it! In this section, we share two more examples from real educators who have hosted Parent Math Nights in their schools.

Lachanda Garrison is a second-grade teacher with the Department of Defense Education Activity overseas. Lachanda was energetic as she shared with us about her Parent Math Nights "Out," an intentional play on the Parent Math Night title. She says,

> We wanted to make it sound like a fun night out! It's a night out for them! We are taking care of you, come and get a free workshop, have your food taken care of, your children are taken care of, and come and learn, no pressure, no stress, and maybe win a prize!

For Lachanda, planning this event with her school's leadership team, though time consuming, is also exciting. She loves that parents can come and get what they need in a fun and relaxing way. And she believes the fun starts with dinner. Her Parent Math Nights "Out" always start with a 50-minute dinner, where parents and their children share food and math conversations across cafeteria tables covered with colorful butcher paper and donned with crayons and markers. The tables are decorated as a workspace to solve problems. Lachanda provides a "Math Conversations Starter" packet of prompts so that parents can engage in sense-making tasks with their children right from the beginning before diving deeper into the content. This also allows Lachanda and the leadership team some time to prepare parents for what to expect the rest of the evening and to provide a brief overview of why math instruction has shifted over the years.

Following dinner, the children head off to the gym with National Honor Society high school student supervisors, Parent Teacher Student Association representatives, and volunteer teachers who lead movement and math activities. The parents head to their first of three 25-minute rotations.

Lachanda and her leadership team built four rotations that align directly to the community's current needs. The last Parent Math Nights "Out" she hosted offered the following stations for parents:

- **A math game station:** fourth and fifth graders in Student Government led this station and taught parents games that will be played in the classroom in upcoming units. Parents then got to make and take the game home to play with their children.
- **A technology station:** an instructional technology specialist led this station, which gave parents an opportunity to learn about math applications and technology used in the classroom and at home.
- **A primary instructional station:** teachers led this station and provided parents instruction on how addition and subtraction is taught from kindergarten to Grade 2.
- **An intermediate instructional station:** teachers led this station and provided parents instruction on how multiplication and division is taught from Grades 3 to 5.

In both of the instructional stations, parents learned about the vertical progression of the models and strategies students use and how we teach conceptually before we generalize shortcuts. Parents could choose which stations most directly applied to their needs and were able to attend both the primary and intermediate sessions if they had children who spanned grade bands, something many parents have mentioned as important in past workshops we have led. Following the three sets of rotations, the children reconvened with their parents for a raffle of prizes before heading home.

In Lachanda's case, her Parent Math Nights were directly built on the needs of her very own community. She and the leadership team recognized that this event would require lots of hands on deck. She strategically sought help from students in the National Honor Society and the Student Council/Government for more support. Lachanda also knew that attendance would suffer if childcare were not provided.

However, she wasn't interested in hosting a Family Math Night because her community needs functioned around deepening parent understanding of the math content and trajectory. Thus, she and the leadership team had to figure out a way to make it so that students could still attend.

Looking for sample Parent Math Night schedules? Here is a summary of Lachanda's Parent Math Night and another event example.

Parent Math Night Possible Schedules	
Lachanda's Parent Math Night	Another Parent Math Night Example
5:00–5:50 Dinner	5:30–6:00 Dinner available
6:00–6:25 Rotation 1	6:00–6:25 Welcome, Presentation
6:30–6:55 Rotation 2	6:30–7:10 Workshop 1
7:00–7:25 Rotation 3	7:15–7:55 Workshop 2
7:25–7:30 Closure and Raffle	7:55–8:00 Closure

Chris Pohlman, a math coach in Nebraska, also acknowledges that parent attendance can vary without the proper structures in place. In Chris's case, she noticed an attributable increase in attendance at her district's Parent Math Nights when the district pushed out an automatic call the night before the event. Because her Parent Math Nights were a *district initiative* around informing parents about today's math, the districtwide automatic call was useful. For schools hosting events that are not districtwide, we suggest implementing the same idea, but only to the parents of the particular school.

The initiative in Chris's district was a grand effort that included offering quarterly Parent Math Nights. Each event lasted 1 hour and focused on previewing the upcoming math content to be taught at each grade level, from kindergarten through eighth grade. She said,

> *We heard a lot from parents that they didn't understand the math their kids were bringing home. Math that was not procedural was frustrating. Our goal was how can we provide something to families that will help parents understand and, in the long run, help us*

because then they're not coming to teachers and saying, "Why are you doing math this way?" or "That's not how I learned it." We wanted to be sure that parents have opportunities to see why we're doing it this way.

With over 60 elementary schools in the district, it is a structural challenge to ensure that all schools are providing equitable opportunities for parents. Chris shared that lots of their schools have hosted Family Math Nights in the past where families and their kids would come together to share in math experiences. But not all schools offered this type of parental support, and based on what the district had been hearing from parents, parents needed more instructional support. Chris added,

*We felt this was an opportunity to include **all** schools districtwide with a focus on teaching parents and giving them support, not kids coming and doing fun math things, but really about parents learning math.*

With a districtwide mission in place, math coaches from across the district banded together, in collaboration with math supervisors, to make this initiative a success. The leadership team had to be intentional about the design. Each math coach chose one particular grade-level focus and led that one grade-level Parent Math Night all four quarters, with the hope that if parents attended multiple sessions, they would form a trusting relationship that might lead to future support. Given her history as a third-grade math teacher, Chris built presentations specifically designed around the scope and sequence of third-grade content for parents of third graders. When parents came for the first-quarter Parent Math Night, the event was focused only on the content they would see in that quarter. This helped narrow the number of topics of focus so parents could get more deeper content knowledge in 1 hour as opposed to a surface-level overview.

Each session was intentionally designed to focus on one to two major mathematical standards. Parents engaged in activities and problem-solving tasks where they used actual concrete manipulatives their children would be using in school during the corresponding unit (where applicable), then represented their work using pictorial representations, and finally abstracted their work by writing equations or using numbers. Parents were provided with vocabulary reference charts that included visuals and supporting documents that they could refer to as their child learned the content.

TIP!

Stagger grade level–specific offerings like Chris did so parents with multiple children can attend multiple sessions. In Chris's district, they offered two sessions on one night for this purpose. Parents with one child would only attend for 1 hour, while parents with multiple children were able to attend for 2 hours and see two different sessions.

No matter how you choose to host a Parent Math Night, be sure you have thought about the same things you would for a Family Math Night. For example, consider how parents will access the information if they cannot attend or whether translations, translators, and interpreters are needed.

- Consider the name you choose when inviting parents to a Parent Math Night, as that could influence your attendance.

- Involve other educators as much as possible. For coaches or school leaders, these events are a great opportunity to provide job-embedded mathematics professional learning and also empower teachers to be leaders. Set aside common planning time or coaching meetings to help teachers plan a workshop they could lead at a Parent Math Night.

- Provide childcare even if the event is not for children.

- Provide food if held during a typical meal time.

- Survey your community before deciding they need this style of event.

 To download sample resources to support your Parent Math Night, visit **resources.corwin.com/ partneringwithparents/elementary**

Family Math Days and Math Mornings

Family Math Nights and Parent Math Nights typically occur in the evenings. For some communities, that is just not an option. Rosa Serratore, a math coordinator in California, has found offering daytime events to be better for her community. Through her work with the California Math Council, she has run several Family Math Days (which they call "Math Festivals") at her school. Parents and students engage in rotations of math play activities during the school day that parents can then try at home with their children.

In this model, parent volunteers are asked to run tables during the day in a large space, such as a gymnasium or multipurpose room. Each grade level is given 45–60 minutes to engage in the activities at the tables. This provides students an opportunity to play and see the math that is offered before pick-up time, when their parents can then join them in the experience. When pick-up time arrives, teacher volunteers run the stations so the parent volunteers can attend the festival with their children, who Rosa says often lead their parents directly to the tables they found the most exciting earlier in the day. She adds, "If you are in a school district that does not rely heavily on bussing, this is a great option."

Rosa has been working to find alternative ways for her community to engage in math other than coming to the school in the evening. In addition to Math Festivals, she also has run what she calls, "Morning Math." The idea came to her when she saw a second-grade class hosting a classroom literacy event first thing in the morning, where students shared some creative writing assignments with their parents. Rosa was amazed to see how many parents were there for the short, 30-minute event. She decided to see how she could use her informal observation as a way to get more parents involved in their child's math learning. After meeting with her teachers who supported the idea, they advertised to parents that they would be hosting a Morning Math where parents can come see how their children learn math today.

The setup was simple and easy to implement, so long as the teachers felt safe and courageous to partake. After parents dropped off their children at school, the kids settled in their classrooms. Parents congregated in the auditorium to receive a quick front-loading presentation (about 5–10 minutes long) about why they were there, what they would expect to see, and, in particular, what to look for given that math instruction looks different than they likely experienced. Should you choose to host a Morning Math, consider providing parents a small reference sheet for what they should be looking for as they enter the classroom for the event. Look at Figure 6.3 for an example.

Figure 6.3 – Observation Look-Fors for Parents for Morning Math

---

What Should You See During Morning Math?

- A task that requires thinking and is not easy to solve quickly
- A task that has multiple ways to reach the solution
- Students engaged in a routine with which they are familiar
- Students given time to talk with each other
- Students building on each other's ideas and listening carefully to each other
- Students feeling safe making mistakes and taking risks
- The teacher facilitating thoughtful math conversations, but not doing the math for the class

---

After the presentation, parents were then free to head to their child's classroom. Parents sat fishbowl style around the students. Each teacher chose whichever sense-making routine they preferred; parents watched the routine and sometimes even participated as learners. The routines varied. Some teachers conducted Number Talks, while others led a "Which One Doesn't Belong?" The goal was to showcase a short routine (15–25 minutes) that provided parents a glimpse into what teaching and learning math looks like today.

Because class continues after parents leave, it is easy to miss out on important feedback that can inform the next offering. So, consider giving parents a reflection form to fill out to help synthesize what they learned and saw, in addition to gathering their feedback on whether the format and structure worked for your community.

- Offer a *Family Math Festival* during the day if daytime is better for your parents and if the majority of students do not take the bus home.

- Offer "open hours" where parents can feel free to attend class at their convenience, such as the first half-hour of school if you host events like Morning Math, rather than restricting it to one particular date.

- Provide parents with some sort of reflection or handout, even if the event is informal or during the school day.

 To download sample resources to support your Family Math Days and Math Mornings, visit **resources .corwin.com/partneringwithparents/elementary**

Parent Book Clubs

You don't have to be Oprah Winfrey to enjoy a good book club! Many schools have started hosting book clubs for parents and some have found success in providing a structured space for parents to read, learn, and communicate about math. However, just because book clubs may be popular or the idea sounds great does not mean this event will be easy to host or be the right fit for your school community. Be sure to find out if parents in your school or district would be interested in such an event and consider ways to make it the most accessible. Parent book clubs, when designed well, offer parents opportunities to:

- **Learn** about strategies, models, and tools that are commonly used today and why math instruction has changed over time,
- **Understand** how to support mathematics learning at home,
- **Meet** other parents who are learning alongside them to form a support network, and
- **Experience** the math their child is learning so they can better support at home.

Four core wants icon sources: Helpful by appleuzr/iStock.com; Intelligent by PeterSnow/ iStock.com; Confident by Bigmouse108/iStock.com; Familiar by PeterSnow/iStock.com.

Stephanie Rousseau, a math specialist in Massachusetts, was interested in hosting a book club for parents using our book written for parents, *Adding Parents to the Equation*. She thought parents would find it helpful, especially with structured guidance. Instead of assuming what parents needed and wanted, she decided to send out a schoolwide survey before dedicating hours of effort to building the club. Stephanie had never hosted a book club before and was not sure parents would be interested (or have time) for such an endeavor. She sent this initial email blast to all parents:

> *Does the way your child is learning math make you want to pull your hair out or have you looking like this??? We can help! We are considering a parent–teacher book study, using the book* Adding Parents to the Equation *by Hilary Kreisberg and Matthew Beyranevand, which sheds light on the how and why we teach elementary math the way we do. At this time we are trying to gauge interest from the parent community.*
>
> *Would you be interested in participating in a parent–teacher book study group using this book?*
>
> ❏ *Yes, definitely!*
>
> ❏ *Yes, but only if it's online*
>
> ❏ *Not at this time*
>
> *Thank you for your time!*

Notice how the correspondence was short, easy to read, and started with a relatable comment to get parents interested. Stephanie was curious about not only whether parents would be interested but also *how* they would participate (in person versus online). She intentionally designed the one-question survey to attend to both the general interest and format.

The results of Stephanie's initial survey were impressive. As she suspected, parents were craving an opportunity to meet and discuss a book about how to help their child with math. She followed the initial correspondence with the email shown in Figure 6.4, along with a registration link.

Figure 6.4 – Follow-Up Book Club Email

Great news! We generated enough interest to host our parent book club using the book *Adding Parents to the Equation* by Hilary Kreisberg and Matthew Beyranevand, a book that sheds light on the how and why we teach elementary math the way we do.

Why should you participate?

1. If **this video clip** resonates with you at all. [*Note:* The link takes parents to the "Math Is Math" scene in *Incredibles 2* via YouTube: https://www.youtube.com/watch?v=3QtRK7Y2pPU]
2. ONE OF THE AUTHORS will be joining us in our online format to chime in and answer questions.
3. For this very special *first-time* math parent book study, our school will be purchasing the books for everyone who participates!!!
4. It is a very flexible format, primarily utilizing an asynchronous online platform so you can fit it into your busy schedule!

When will it take place?

Begins in early March—exact date TBD. If you can't make the first meeting, we'll arrange for you to get your book a different way. Don't let that stop you!

Where will it take place?

Our first meeting will be at [Name of School] to pick up books and learn about the online platform we'll be using. All future "meetings" will be inside the online platform and we will have an *optional* in-person celebration with your students for our final meeting.

As you can see, once again Stephanie used her convincing writing skills to find ways to encourage parents to attend. She started by relating to how parents currently feel using the "Math Is Math" scene from the *Incredibles 2* movie. She also reached out to us, the authors, ahead of time and asked us to come speak at their first in-person meeting and to participate in the online work and used our agreement as a "selling point" for parents. Additionally, she found funding to be able to increase accessibility by providing every parent their own copy of the book. Finally, she emphasized the relaxed and flexible nature of the event, honoring parents' limited time.

The initial in-person meeting was a huge success. She had 65 parents commit to the book club and on March 11 parents showed up for a 1-hour first session where she introduced the structure of the club, discussed the expectations, and had one of us authors do a 30-minute presentation focused on the "Top Three Facts Every Parent Needs to Know About Today's Math."

Stephanie said to us in a follow-up interview,

> *I think that the high book club attendance really speaks to the need that exists because I'm in my 16th year of teaching math and the questions have not stopped from parents. It has been the same questions: "Why has math changed? What was wrong with how I learned math? How can I best help my child with this 'new math'?" There is still a lot more work to be done.*

Following the in-person meeting, parents were asked to read the Introduction and Chapter 1 in *Adding Parents to the Equation* and begin the online engagement through the use of Flipgrid, an interactive educational technology platform that fosters community through shared video experiences. Stephanie used the accompanying book study guide to generate questions that parents would answer on a weekly basis. The book club culminated with an optional in-person celebration for parents and students at the final meeting.

> ### TIP!
> Find the link to the book study guide for *Adding Parents to the Equation* on the companion website. You can use this guide to help determine what types of questions to ask parents as they read your chosen book. You can also find a list of book club–worthy books or recommended reading for parents.

 Adding Parents to the Equation study guide available for download at **resources.corwin.com/partneringwithparents/elementary**

Laura Vizdos Tomas, a math coach in Florida, also was interested in hosting a book club for parents. Her format was different from Stephanie's approach. Laura opted for in-person sessions so she could use her time with parents to also have them try out some activities from the chosen book and become more comfortable with manipulatives. While restricting events to in-person meetings often sacrifices the number of committed attendees, it also provides an intimate space whereby deeper learning can occur for those who join. Laura was able to cultivate strong relationships with the parents. Many parents even felt empowered to purchase certain manipulatives that could support learning at home, which is the best bang for their buck because now they know how to use them!

Instead of purchasing the books for parents, Laura offered two options: (1) parents could purchase their own books or (2) parents could borrow copies. This move increased access for parents since there was no financial commitment attached. Each session was built on several chapters and was structured so that there was both discussion time among the parents, using the accompanying book study guide as a facilitation tool, and time for parents to play with the math and learn how to use some of the recommended manipulatives from the book at home.

When asked whether she thought hosting the book club was worth her time, given that her attendance was one-tenth of her Family Math Nights, Laura responded:

> *Absolutely! I wouldn't have cared if it was only one person! That's one more person who LEARNED!*

She is right. Look at some of the things parents wrote on their exit tickets from the club, which is direct evidence that parents gained valuable experiences from participating:

- *I am not going to show him how I learned it. I will talk to his teacher so she can guide me through it next time.*

- *This is wonderful. I feel like I am learning the skills to assist with math in a fun way, not as a grumpy mom!*

- *I will say numbers in their whole beauty. Instead of saying* one thirty-two, *I will say* one hundred thirty-two.

- *I will accept ways of solving a problem besides "my way."*

- *I will encourage and praise the process and effort.*

- *I will say* regrouping *instead of* borrowing.

Dr. Molly Rawding, who we mentioned earlier for her Family Math Night work, also says she sees incredible value in hosting a parent book club. Molly's approach was slightly different from both Stephanie and Laura's in that she first ran the book study *with teachers* to build their capacity and enhance their professional learning community. She chose the book *Table Talk Math: A Practical Guide to Bringing Math Into Everyday Conversations* by John Stevens (2017) because it connected directly to the focus of play and conversations at home from their Family Math Nights. The feedback from teachers was very positive and many felt it would be helpful if parents, too, read this book so they could share in the experience. Molly agreed, especially because the book is easy to read and offers simple and manageable things parents can do at home, such as doing less telling and more listening.

Molly took the suggestion and co-planned the book club event with another math specialist from a different school in the same district. She advises any person who is starting a new event from scratch to always collaborate with others to build it; collaboration also ensures that the event goes beyond just one school's set of parents. This was Molly's first year running a book club. Like Laura, she sees tremendous value in offering a variety of opportunities for parents to engage in deepening their understanding of math and how to help their children at home. She says,

> *Things start small and events like these build momentum over time. Even if it's just a handful of parents to start, it's important for those families, and then those parents will share with other people in the community. This is just the first step.*

Book clubs are a great way to engage parents in deeper thinking around the math their children are learning and to create a network for adults—like a professional learning community—so they can feel safe asking questions and learning together.

- Consider picking a book that is available in multiple languages and as an audiobook to increase accessibility.
- Try to use a book that comes with a facilitation guide. This will save you time by having prescribed questions and areas of focus.
- Pick a book you have read. Just because a book is newly popular doesn't mean it aligns to your school's shared vision. Read the book to anticipate areas where parents might struggle or to find specific sections that align nicely to your school's work.
- Do you have another event happening before the book club? Hand out flyers at that event to drum up interest.

 To download sample resources to support your Parent Book Clubs, visit **resources.corwin.com/ partneringwithparents/elementary**

Mystery Mathematicians

Have you ever hosted a "Mystery Reader" session in your classroom or at your school? Or perhaps you have been a Mystery Reader for a classroom or even your own child's school. If you are not familiar with this event, most elementary school websites define Mystery Readers as special guests who come into the classroom to read a story to the children. Often, these guests share three to five facts about themselves that the teacher then posts before their arrival so students can act like detectives to guess who the Mystery Reader is.

To understand how popular this event is in elementary schools, a simple search engine search for "mystery reader" populates 276,000,000 hits, with pages and pages about how to do this in your classroom or school and teacher websites inviting families to come read a book to their class and partake in this fun event. Comparatively, a simple search engine search for "mystery mathematician" populates 3,440,000 hits, with no page to be found about entering a classroom.

In fact, in searching about the goals behind Mystery Readers, we found one that is commonly written on many school websites. It reads,

> At [Name of School], we strive to foster a love of reading both in school and at home. The aim of "Mystery Reader" is to show children that adults love reading too so we would like to invite parents, grandparents or other family members to come into their child's class to read a children's story.

We have noticed in our experiences that schools often take a literacy-centric focus. Our goal is to help uncover ways we can engage in mathematics in similar ways we do with literacy. Perhaps in addition to a Mystery Reader, you also host a Mystery Mathematician, Mystery Scientist, Mystery Engineer, or Mystery Artist. Or simply invite a Mystery Guest to your school and that guest can be any of the above. We have rewritten the school's invitation with this focus in mind:

> At [Name of School], we strive to foster a love of **learning** both in school and at home. The aim of "Mystery **Guests**" is to show children that adults **are also still learning and that they use what they have learned to help them**. We would like to invite **all caregivers**, including parents, guardians, grandparents, or other family members to come into their child's class to **help us expand our perspectives. Here are some examples of things you can share: play a game and look for content connections, teach a trick and uncover the math and science behind it, read a book, and more.**

Benefits of Organizing Mystery Mathematicians

- Students learn traits mathematicians exhibit,
- Students begin to see themselves as mathematicians,
- Students see math as joyful and fun,
- Students see mathematicians as diverse human beings,
- Parents learn to see themselves as mathematicians, and
- Parents see that math is more than doing procedures or getting answers.

If you type "mathematician" into a search engine, often what you find are a series of images of mostly older, white males, most of whom never lived in our lifetime. You also likely see very serious, stoic faces or people's brows angled as if the math is making their brain hurt. Unfortunately, these are the stereotypes that pervade our society and still influence how many children view math and mathematicians. Mystery Mathematician is one way of breaking through these stereotypes.

By creating a fun, mystery experience led by real people from the community, students and parents get to see that math is quite joyful and does not at all resemble the images they may see in other media (Figure 6.5).

Figure 6.5 – Mystery Readers and Mystery Mathematicians

Mystery Readers	Mystery Mathematicians
• Read a book. • Answer questions about how they use reading in the workplace or home. • Share their favorite book. • Read the beginning of a story and have the class finish the story with their own ending.	• Play a game and identify the math within a game or how math can be used to help. • Teach the class how they learned a specific procedure that's being studied and compare it to the strategies learned so far. • Write a puzzle or riddle for the class to uncover. • Create a mini escape room and discuss the problem-solving and logic required to solve each step. • Make up their own math game. • Tie the history of math into the topic being studied.

Mystery Mathematicians is also an excellent chance to encourage parents who come from other countries or backgrounds to share how they learned specific mathematics topics. Imagine how powerful it would be for a parent from Latin America to come and show how they learned to write division, as shown on the right side of Figure 6.6.

Figure 6.6 – Differences in Notation of Algorithms

Though this is not the notation we learn to write in the United States, there are clear parallels between our methods and more traditionally, the standard algorithm for division. Students could analyze the similarities and differences by making noticings and wonderings. This opportunity exposes students to alternative notations that they might encounter, and it teaches them to show appreciation for various cultural and global differences.

The first step is to invite parents and be clear about what the event entails. See Figure 6.7 for an example invitation teachers or school leaders can send to parents.

Figure 6.7

Example Mystery Mathematician Invitation

Dear Families,

One of our goals this year is to help students see themselves as mathematicians.

Who is a mathematician? A mathematician is . . .

- A person who does mathematics,
- A person who studies mathematics, and/or
- An expert in mathematics.

YOU are a mathematician.

To diversify our children's experiences, we want them to see that their very own community engages in joyful math and that people from every culture, gender, and background are mathematicians. Since you are a mathematician, we need your help!

Just like we have Mystery Readers, we would like to have Mystery Mathematicians—people who can teach us some math, play a game that involves math with us, or share how they use math every day or in their job. Perhaps you grew up in a different country and learned math differently? We'd love to see how you learned it and compare it to what we are studying.

→ **Speak a language other than English?** No worries! Your child or a translator will assist.

→ **Can't make it into the classroom?** No worries! We are happy to video conference with you or you could prerecord a video that we show in class at a later time.

→ **Interested, but can't think of what to share?** No worries! We are happy to work with you to share something related to what we are currently learning.

Please check the appropriate box:

❏ I am interested! Please let me know how I can help.
❏ I am not interested at this time.

 Available for download at **resources.corwin.com/partneringwithparents/elementary**

Once parents have indicated interest, collaborate to determine what works for your classroom and group of students. No matter what, be sure the time together is joyful and fun!

- Reach out to parents if they do not volunteer.
- Encourage parents from other countries to share differences in the way they learned mathematics compared to their children.
- Be flexible and encourage any mode of participation, even if a parent feels most comfortable sharing a game or experience by writing about it. Read it aloud to the class and honor that parent's contribution.
- Invite parents to be Mystery Mathematicians after you have begun to build strong relationships with parents and cultivated trust around mathematics.

 To download sample resources to support your Mystery Mathematicians, visit **resources.corwin.com/partneringwithparents/elementary**

PUTTING IT ALL TOGETHER

In this chapter, we explored various events that schools or classrooms might host that involve parents. We identified ways to elevate events nonspecific to mathematics to offer mathematics information, and we shared powerful anecdotes from real educators and school leaders about ways to plan and enact numerous mathematics-focused events. Regardless of the type of event, there are many things to consider when thinking about making an event accessible.

General Accessibility Tips for Hosting Parent Events

- Have a translator or interpreter, if needed (if you use a registration form, include a section asking parents if this accommodation is needed).
- Caption all videos you show face-to-face and provide for parents who did not attend.
- Use a microphone when speaking to a group, even if the group feels small.
- Have a plan for parents who won't or can't attend. Consider how you will provide them access to the outcomes for each session in a timely fashion and how you will collect data on whether they accessed the materials and found them useful. Here are some examples:
  - Record the whole-group or introductory sessions so that you can develop a webinar that gets posted to the school or district's math website.
  - Post all handouts on the school or district math website with a short video or annotation detailing about the handouts.
  - Post an optional survey link on all handouts and websites for those who did not attend to fill out after they have watched or read the materials.
- If possible and appropriate, host the event off the school campus in a "neutral" space such as a public library. Sometimes this can increase the attendance rate, as it feels less academic for those who might have an aversion to school.
- Offer childcare in some fashion and provide food.

FREQUENTLY ASKED QUESTIONS

Q There are so many events we can offer that I have never even thought of! How do you prioritize which to offer?

A Each and every school/district has their own "must-haves." From there, you can decide which event is a "nice to have." Typically, parent conferences and curriculum nights are must-haves. Beyond that, it is up to you to decide which event(s) would best suit the needs of your parents. We always suggest surveying parents to find out: take the guesswork out of it and don't just choose what is the easiest or most convenient. Send a simple survey that tells parents your school is planning to offer a math-focused event to support parents' needs and you need to know which format most interests them. Provide a brief description of what each would look like and use the results to dictate which event you try!

Q Planning these events sounds like a huge task and time commitment. How long does it take for these types of events to be put together?

A Depending on the event, it totally can be! Some events require more time commitment than others. For example, Mystery Mathematicians, Morning Math, or Parent Book Club events require far less planning and setup than a Family Math Night or Parent Math Night. In our interviews, some educators shared with us that planning the Family Math Nights or the Parent Math Nights felt like planning a wedding. You have to plan not only the content but also the entire setup (e.g., Where do people sit or stand? What do they get when they are greeted? How do they know where to go?). In our experience, it can take months to put together a successful Parent Math Night or Family Math Night. It can take a few weeks to prepare for a parent book club.

APPLY IT! TEACHER ACTIVITIES

How Will You Improve Your Parent Events?

1.   Which events on our list does your school already employ? What considerations from this chapter are new to you that you could bring back to the event organizers?

2.   Which events on our list has your school not tried yet? What would need to happen to make these events possible?

3.   What are your goals for engaging parents in math-specific or nonmath-specific events? Which of the parent events we mentioned would align most with those goals?

4.   What do the parents in your school community need? How do you know?

APPLY IT! SCHOOL LEADER ACTIVITIES

How Will You Improve Your Parent Events?

1.   Which events on our list does your school already employ? What considerations from this chapter are new to you that you could make sure are in place?

2.   Which events on our list has your school not tried yet? What would need to happen to make these events possible?

3.   Which events do you believe will have the greatest impact on parents in your community? Why?

Apply It! icon source: PeterSnow/iStock.com.

Shifting the Narrative

*I always wondered why somebody doesn't do something
about that.
Then I realized I was somebody.*
— Lily Tomlin

Well, you made it to the end, or should we say the beginning? It is now time to take all that you have read and continue, or start, your journey toward helping parents feel helpful, intelligent, confident, and familiar with the language as you partner in their child's mathematics education—their four core wants. Let's take a moment to reflect on our journey together.

In Chapter 1, we asked you to step into parents' shoes to understand how they feel and why they feel the way they do about mathematics teaching and learning today—what they consider to be the "new math." Many parents want to support the instructional methods their children's teachers use, but they just do not know how. They shared frustration, confusion, anxiety, and stress with us as we listened to their stories. What we learned is that we need to do a better job as an educational system educating parents.

Chapter 2 examined what parents want and need to know, particularly about today's mathematics instruction in general. Helping parents understand that mathematics instruction evolves, just like everything else, allows parents to recognize that mathematics is a science. We shared the need for parents to understand that mathematics is not a gene that they pass down to their children; rather, math is something everyone can do with effort. We also shared ways to encourage parents to recognize that the math we teach children today is meant to prepare them for their future.

Chapter 3 dove into schoolwide structures needed to promote successful mathematics. We established why there needs to be clear and consistent messaging related to roles and responsibilities, homework, report cards, and communication. We provided suggestions for how to prioritize and develop a schoolwide commitment to addressing parents' needs. We also discussed how to approach schoolwide consensus if a building or district has yet to do so.

In Chapter 4, we explored how to communicate with parents. We discussed what makes written communication with parents effective, reflected on how you can enhance your communication about mathematics with parents, and reviewed various methods and tools used to communicate with parents.

Chapter 5 built on Chapter 4 by offering what specifically should be included in communication with parents. We showcased three levels of communication and offered resources to support each level, including surveys, how to analyze the data collected from surveys to inform future communication, letters about how and why we teach math the way we do today, and how to make communication two way between educators and parents.

In Chapter 6, we offered many ways to involve parents in experiencing and learning about 21st century mathematics teaching. Anecdotes from real educators gave readers a glimpse into how one might design parent events to meet the needs of their own community. Resources and templates were provided to offer you a starting point as you consider hosting any of the events.

So what does it all look like once parents are positioned as partners? Let's return to the scenario from the Introduction where the child was puzzled over a homework assignment and asked the parent for help. The first task was to solve 13 × 6 using an area model. A parent who views themselves as a partner would not say, "What the heck is an area model? That's not how I learned how to do it." Instead the parent would ask, "Can you show me what you've done so far? What exactly are you struggling with?" The child may respond, "Nothing." The parent then might ask, "What do you know about 13 × 6? Is it greater than or less than 100? How do you know?" followed by "Can you use 10 × 6 to help you get started?" If the child has some work to show and responds by sharing with the parent how they started, the parent might ask specific questions about the work (e.g., calculation errors or placement of numbers) or have the child to start anew using the same questions previously mentioned. Ultimately, the parent may suggest that the child put a sticky note on the homework and write to the teacher where they struggled. All of this is now possible because the child's parent has been informed. The parent has received a beginning of the year letter about why mathematics instruction is different today than in the past, had a strengths-based phone call with the teacher, clarified their role in homework, and received a unit overview letter outlining what area models are and what questions to ask their child at home to support learning. Among other experiences, this parent is now well equipped to be a partner in their child's mathematics education.

Now take a moment to reflect on your entire experience. Think about what you will do differently and how you will challenge other educators to band together to shift the parent narrative. How will you apply and use what you have learned in this book to empower parents and change the paradigm? Use the reflection box on the next page to organize your thoughts.

Reflect

Reflection Questions	My Thoughts and Reflections
What is one action step you will focus on tomorrow?	
What is one action step you will focus on next week?	
What is one action step you will focus on a month from now?	
Who will you collaborate with to materialize these action steps?	

OUR TOP EIGHT WAYS TO SUPPORT PARENTS IN MATHEMATICS

What better way to conclude our book than to sum up the learning with a list of ways to prepare parents for 21st century mathematics teaching and learning? While some of the following suggestions require more resources or a greater time commitment than others, the effort is worth the reward. Partnering with parents in their child's mathematics education will undoubtedly have positive benefits on the students, as you saw in the revisited vignette. Moreover, by positioning parents as partners, they will have a better understanding of their child's current and future mathematical development and will be able to communicate with other parents, helping to shift the narrative.

1. **View Parents as Partners.** Parents want to help their children and be part of the solution, but they usually do not know how. They need school leaders and teachers to partner with them to provide explicit information about what role they should be playing in their child's mathematical development.

2. **Communicate Often.** In order for parents to be able to best support their children, they need to know how and when to intervene. Communicate with parents as often as possible about their child's mathematics progress and offer specific suggestions that parents can immediately put into place.

3. **Use "Parentspeak."** As educators, we are well versed in educational lingo and abbreviations, but parents who are not educators are not. Be sure your communication is written so that it is easily readable by a sixth-grade student and use visuals to support the writing.

4. **Use Strengths-Based Language.** When communicating with parents, always speak from a strengths-based perspective. This means focus on what a student *can do* and *has done* rather than what they can't do or haven't done. We want to model for parents positive language that focuses on assets, not deficits, so that parents can use our examples to speak about mathematics and student work at home.

5. **Focus on Schoolwide Consensus.** For true long-term success, consistency and buy-in from all stakeholders is key with regard to specific structures. Policies about homework and grading, along with which tools used to communicate and frequency of communication, are some of the areas to strive for consistency as a school.

6. **Use Formative Assessments With Parents.** Just as it is critical to get to know your students, the same effort should be made with parents. How often and what kinds of communications are parents looking for? What are their perceptions of math and how do their perceptions impact their child's vision of mathematics? Use surveys and other formative assessment techniques to provide you much needed information that you can use to inform your communication and instruction.

7. **Host Math-Specific Parent Events.** Identify which types of events are most needed and wanted among your community. Then, plan and prepare to host these events to support parent learning. There are many different options for events and even if events are small to start, informing some parents about how we teach math is better than none.

8. **Embed Mathematics Within Events Nonspecific to Math.** There are some events that are not math specific but bring many parents to the school. Use these events to embed mathematics support in some fashion so if those are the only events parents attend, they get some information about mathematics.

It is our hope that with this book, you will now be able to help parents go from this:

> *There's very limited information that comes home . . . so she comes home with a worksheet and there's one example . . . and I'm trying to follow the work they're showing you, but I don't understand how they're going from Point A to Point B the way they want you to. I don't have any other information to look at to help other than the little problem at the top of the worksheet.*
>
> — Parent of a Second Grader

To this:

> *I am able to support my child with both the math homework that is assigned as well as the understanding of the concepts. We have developed a strong communication with her teacher and I feel informed with what is occurring now and coming up soon in the class.*
>
> — Parent of a Second Grader

In the words of Maya Angelou,

> *I did then what I knew best, when I knew better, I did better.*

How will you help change the narrative?

References

Bembenutty, H. (2011). The last word: An interview with Harris Cooper—research, policies, tips, and current perspectives on homework. *Journal of Advanced Academics, 22*(2), 340–349.

Boaler, J. (2015). *What's math got to do with it? How teachers and parents can transform mathematics learning and inspire success.* New York, NY: Penguin.

Boaler, J. (2016). *Mathematical mindsets: Unleashing students' potential through creative math, inspiring messages and innovative teaching.* San Francisco, CA: John Wiley & Sons.

Chiu, M., & Xihua, Z. (2008). Family and motivation effects on mathematics achievement: Analyses of students in 41 countries. *Learning and Instruction, 18*(4), 321–336.

Cooper, H. (1989). *Homework.* New York, NY: Longman.

Dweck, C. S. (2006). *Mindset: The new psychology of success.* New York, NY: Ballantine Books.

Dweck, C. S. (2015, September 22). Carol Dweck revisits the 'growth mindset.' *Education Week, 35*(5),20, 24. Retrieved from https://www.edweek.org/ew/articles/2015/09/23/carol-dweck-revisits-the-growth-mindset.html

Edwards, P., & Compton-Lilly, C. (2016). *New ways to engage parents: Strategies and tools for teachers and leaders, K–12.* New York, NY: Teachers College Press.

Fan, W., & Williams, C. M. (2010). The effects of parental involvement on students' academic self-efficacy, engagement and intrinsic motivation. *Educational Psychology, 30*(1), 53–74.

Finkel, D. (2016, February 17). Five principles of extraordinary math teaching. *TEDx Talk.* https://www.youtube.com/watch?v=ytVneQUA5-c&fbclid=IwAR2HRr03p50wSk4PtrRNgJw73JnuAV7IT3JOEZXoLgEZKdPOKNBQ6hWkxA0

Fosnot, C. T., & Dolk, M. (2001). *Young mathematicians at work: Constructing multiplication and division.* Westport, CT: Heinemann.

Gauvreau, A., & Sandall, S. (2019). Using mobile technologies to communicate with parents and caregivers. *Young Exceptional Children, 22*(3), 115–126.

Henderson, A., Mapp, K., Johnson, V., & Davies, D. (2007). *Beyond the bake sale: The essential guide to family-school partnerships.* New York, NY: The New Press.

Jay, T., Rose, J., & Simmons, B. (2018). Why is parental involvement in children's mathematics learning hard? Parental perspectives on their role supporting children's learning. *SAGE Open, 8*(2). https://doi.org/10.1177/2158244018775466

Karp, K. S., Dougherty, B. J., & Bush, S. B. (2020). *The math pact, elementary: Achieving instructional coherence within and across grades.* Thousand Oaks, CA: Corwin.

Kobett, B., & Karp, K. (2020). *Strengths-based teaching and learning in mathematics.* Thousand Oaks, CA: Corwin.

Kraft, M. A., & Dougherty, S. M. (2013). The effect of teacher–family communication on student engagement: Evidence from a randomized field experiment. *Journal of Research on Educational Effectiveness, 6*(3), 199–222.

Kreisberg, H., & Beyranevand, M. L. (2019). *Adding parents to the equation: Understanding your child's elementary school math.* Lanham, MD: Rowman & Littlefield.

Mapp, K., Carver, I., & Lander, J. (2017). *Powerful partnerships: A teacher's guide to engaging families for student success.* New York, NY: Scholastic.

Meyer, D. (2011). *The three acts of a mathematical story.* Retrieved from https://blog.mrmeyer.com/2011/the-three-acts-of-a-mathematical-story/

National Council of Teachers of Mathematics and Hunt Institute. (2015, April 15). *NCTM Mathematics Video Series: Parents Supporting Mathematics Learning.* Retrieved from https://hunt-institute.org/resources/2015/04/nctm-mathematics-video-series-parents-supporting-mathematics-learning/

National Education Association. (2015). *Research spotlight on homework.* Retrieved from http://ftp.arizonaea.org/tools/16938.htm

National Governors Association Center for Best Practices, Council of Chief State School Officers. (2010). *Common Core State Standards for Mathematics.* Washington, DC: Author.

National Parent Teacher Association. (2016). *Resolution on homework: Quality over quantity.* Retrieved from https://www.pta.org/home/advocacy/ptas-positions/Individual-PTA-Resolutions/Homework-Quality-Over-Quantity

NCSM. (2020). *Essential actions series: Framework for leadership in mathematics education.* Retrieved from https://www.mathedleadership.org/ncsm-essential-actions-series/

Pew Research Center. (2019, June 12). *Mobile fact sheet: Mobile phone ownership over time.* Retrieved from https://www.pewresearch.org/internet/fact-sheet/mobile/

ProLiteracy. (2018). *Adult literacy facts.* Retrieved May 3, 2020 from https://proliteracy.org/Adult-Literacy-Facts

Ricci, M. C., & Lee, M. (2016). *Mindsets for parents: Strategies to encourage growth mindsets in kids.* Waco, TX: Prufrock Press.

SanGiovanni, J. J., Katt, S., & Dykema, K. J. (2020). *Productive math struggle: A 6-point action plan for fostering perseverance.* Thousand Oaks, CA: Corwin.

Sheppard, L. D., & Vernon, P. A. (2008). Intelligence and speed of information-processing: A review of 50 years of research, *Journal of Personality and Individual Differences, 44*(3), 535–551.

Stevens, J. (2017). *Table talk math: A practical guide to bringing math into everyday conversations*. San Diego, CA: Dave Burgess Consulting.

Tanton, J. (2018). Just teach my kid the <adjective> math. *Medium*. Retrieved from https://medium.com/q-e-d/just-teach-my-kid-the-expletive-math-fb6f495be906

Transforming Education. (2014). What is a growth mindset, and why does it matter? *Growth Mindset Toolkit*. Retrieved from https://www.transformingeducation.org/growth-mindset-toolkit/

U.S. Census Bureau. (2018a). Presence and types of Internet subscriptions in household: 1-year estimates. *American Community Survey*. Retrieved from https://data.census.gov/cedsci/table?q=B28002%3A%20PRESENCE%20AND%20TYPES%20OF%20INTERNET%20SUBSCRIPTIONS%20IN%20HOUSEHOLD&hidePreview=true&table=B28002&tid=ACSDT1Y2018.B28002&lastDisplayedRow=12&moe=true&t=Telephone,%20Computer,%20and%20Internet%20Access&g=0100000US&y=2018

U.S. Census Bureau. (2018b). Types of computers and Internet subscriptions. *American Community Survey*. Retrieved from https://data.census.gov/cedsci/table?q=smartphone&hidePreview=false&tid=ACSST1Y2018.S2801&vintage=2018

U.S. Department of Education. (2017). *Highlights of the 2017 U.S. PIAAC Results Web Report (NCES 2020–777)*. Washington, DC: U.S. Department of Education, Institute of Education Sciences, National Center for Education Statistics. Retrieved from https://nces.ed.gov/surveys/piaac/current_results.asp

U.S. Department of Health and Human Services, Centers for Medicare and Medicaid Services. (2010). Part 7: Using readability formulas: A cautionary note. *Toolkit for Making Written Material Clear and Effective*. Retrieved May 3, 2020 from https://www.cms.gov/Outreach-and-Education/Outreach/WrittenMaterialsToolkit/

Vitale, J. S. (2020). *Student perceptions of mathematical mindset influences* (Publication No. 294) [Doctoral dissertation, University of New England]. UNE Theses and Dissertations. Retrieved from https://dune.une.edu/theses/294

Walker, J. M., Hoover-Dempsey, K. V., Whetsel, D. R., & Green, C. L. (2004). *Parental involvement in homework: A review of current research and its implications for teachers, after school program staff, and parent leaders*. Cambridge, MA: Harvard Family Research Project. Retrieved from https://archive.globalfrp.org/publications-resources/browse-our-publications/parental-involvement-in-homework-a-review-of-current-research-and-its-implications-for-teachers-after-school-program-staff-and-parent-leaders

World Economic Forum. (2016). *The Future of Jobs Report: Employment, skills and workforce strategy for the fourth industrial revolution.* Retrieved from https://reports.weforum.org/future-of-jobs-2016/

World Economic Forum. (2018). *The Future of Jobs Report.* Retrieved from https://www.weforum.org/reports/the-future-of-jobs-report-2018/

Index

CORWIN
A SAGE Publishing Company

CORWIN HAS ONE MISSION: to enhance education through intentional professional learning.

We build long-term relationships with our authors, educators, clients, and associations who partner with us to develop and continuously improve the best evidence-based practices that establish and support lifelong learning.

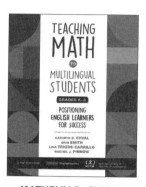
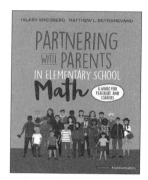

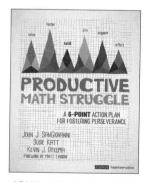

KAREN S. KARP, BARBARA J. DOUGHERTY, SARAH B. BUSH

A schoolwide solution for students' mathematics success

Elementary, Middle School, High School

JENNIFER M. BAY-WILLIAMS, JOHN J. SANGIOVANNI

Because fluency is so much more than basic facts and algorithms

Grades K–8

MARGARET (PEG) SMITH, VICTORIA BILL, MIRIAM GAMORAN SHERIN, MICHAEL D. STEELE

Take a deeper dive into understanding the five practices—anticipating, monitoring, selecting, sequencing, and connecting—for facilitating productive mathematical conversations in your classrooms

Elementary, Middle School, High School

JOHN HATTIE, DOUGLAS FISHER, NANCY FREY, JOHN ALMARODE, LINDA M. GOJAK, SARA DELANO MOORE, WILLIAM MELLMAN, JOSEPH ASSOF, KATERI THUNDER

Powerful, precision teaching through intentionally designed, guided, collaborative, and independent learning

Grades K–2, 3–5, 6–8, 9–12

CORWIN